M²S PUZZLE

				1			3	
						8		5
	3		8	9			2	
		2	8	1	6			
7			3	5	7			6
			4	9	2			3
	4					7	6	
			7					
1	7				6		9	

STEVEN C. BENTON

iUniverse books may be ordered through booksellers or by contacting:

iUniverse
1663 Liberty Drive
Bloomington, IN 47403
www.iuniverse.com
844-349-9409

Because of the dynamic nature of the Internet, any web addresses or links contained in this book may have changed since publication and may no longer be valid. The views expressed in this work are solely those of the author and do not necessarily reflect the views of the publisher, and the publisher hereby disclaims any responsibility for them.

Any people depicted in stock imagery provided by Getty Images are models,
and such images are being used for illustrative purposes only.
Certain stock imagery © Getty Images.

ISBN: 978-1-6632-3143-7 (sc)
ISBN: 978-1-6632-3142-0 (e)

Print information available on the last page.

iUniverse rev. date: 11/16/2021

Magic Square Sudoku M²S Puzzle

M²S is a puzzle which incorporates 3x3 magic squares into a Sudoku matrix. It is a puzzle inside a puzzle. Magic squares are a 3x3 matrix where the sum of the rows, columns and main diagonals all add up to the same number. In the case of a 3x3 matrix, the sum of the number is 15. In Sudoku, where the rows and columns contain the numbers 1-9, the cells in the magic square matrix can be used as clues to aid in solving the larger Sudoku puzzle.

A Magic Square

8	1	6
3	5	7
4	9	2

M²S Puzzle

8	1	6						
3	5	7						
4	9	2						
						2	7	6
						9	5	1
						4	3	8

Directions for solving a M²S puzzle. In M²S some of the clues come from three partial 3x3 magic squares. The first step is to locate and solve the 3x3 magic square. Then solve the Sudoku matrix using the 3x3 magic squares as clues. It is not necessary to supply all of the numbers in the 3x3 magic squares. In addition, to simplify some of the puzzles, other clues not in the 3x3 magic square can be included. When completing the puzzle, the 3x3 magic squares will be contained in the body of the Sudoku puzzle. There can be a maximum of three 3x3 magic squares in the Sudoku matrix because, in 3x3 magic squares, the middle cell of the 3x3 magic square must be a 5. Therefore, if two 3x3 magic squares are in the same row or column, then that row or column in the Sudoku matrix will have more than one 5. This violates a rule of solving a Sudoku puzzle.

M²S Puzzle 1 ♦

8		6			7			5
3				1			4	2
		2	3					
		9	8		4	5		1
2						3	6	
		5	6		2		8	
					1	2		4
		1	4				5	
			5		3	6		

M²S Puzzle 2 ♦

6	7		1					
	5	9	2	4			6	7
					9		2	1
		7	8		6			5
	1				7		4	
	8			9		1	7	
		1				2	9	
	2			6				3
5			7		4	6		8

M²S Puzzle 3 ♦

2		6	1		5	4		
9	5			4				7
			6	7			2	1
7			8		6			5
6		9			7		4	
		3		9		1		
1				8			9	4
	2		9		1	7		3
				2				8

M²S Puzzle 4 ♦

4	9					3	8	
3		7	1			9		6
				9				7
9			5		7	6		
			6		9	7		3
6		5						4
	4			7	6			9
7			9			4		2
					8		7	

M²S Puzzle 5 ♦

	1	6	3		2		4	
3	5		1		4	9		6
				6			8	
			5	2			1	8
	2				9	7		3
6		5		1			9	
5		1	2				3	
	8	3			1			2
2			4		8	1		

M²S Puzzle 6 ♦

				7		8	3	
	8		9				6	
		9	3				7	
9			5		7	6		8
1	2			4				
				1	3	2		
8	1	6	9		2			7
	5				4			6
4								1

M²S Puzzle 7 ♦

			5			6		
		8		4	9	7		3
6			8				9	
5		1		7	6		3	9
					1	4		2
2		9	4	3				
	1	6					4	7
	5		1			9		
4			7	6			8	1

M²S Puzzle 8 ♦

	4	7		1			9	
		6	3		7			
	8			9		7	6	
		8	9					
			1					9
	9	4	6	7			1	
				4		2		6
	6			8	3			1
1	7		2		9	4		

M²S Puzzle 9 ♦

7			8		6			2
	2			5			8	
	8	3			2	7		
8		6	9		4			7
		7				6		
4			6	7			1	3
9		8		4	1	2		6
	6			8			5	
		1	2					

M²S Puzzle 10 ♦

	7		8		3	2		
				4			5	3
	3	9		2	7	6		8
	4		2				3	
	8		9			4		2
9		2	4				7	5
	1	8						
	5		1		4		2	6
2							8	

M²S Puzzle 11 ♦

	1	6				9		5
			9		6	8		
	9	2					7	6
			7	6		2		
		1		2	8	7		3
7	2		5		3			8
	7	9	8			5	2	
				5	9			
	3	5		7			8	9

M²S Puzzle 12 ♦

	7	9	8		4			1
2		8					6	
1			6		2	4		
	8		7		1		9	
9		1		2		7		
		4					1	8
	1						3	
3		7	9		6	8		2
4		2		8	5			6

M²S Puzzle 13 ♦

			8		6	2		
9	2	6					8	
	8		4	9		5		7
	1						2	5
7		3	1	2		9		
		4		7			1	
	3		5			6		2
		2		8			5	9
	7			6	9		3	

M²S Puzzle 14 ♦

7	4		8		6			2
			3			1		
1		3		9	2	7		
8			9		4		2	
3	5	7						9
		2		7		8		3
			2		9	4		8
2		4		8	3		5	
9	3							6

M²S Puzzle 15 ♦

	4		6		2	8		9
3				5	9		6	2
		2	8			1	7	
	7		3	1		2		4
		1	9			7	5	
	3	9		2	5			8
6		8	2			5		
7			4		1	9	2	
				6	7			

M²S Puzzle 16 ♦

1		5		7	2	8		
	8	7	1				6	2
9				3	4	1		5
		6					9	
8				4		7		3
	3			2	5	6		
	1				3		4	
7		3		8			2	
2	9		5	6		3		1

M²S Puzzle 17 ♦

8		6		4	7			5
		7	9				4	
4	9			8				6
		5			2	4		9
		8	1	5		3	6	
6	7			3	4			1
	2	4	5				1	6
		1		2	8	7		3
	8			6	1		9	

M²S Puzzle 18 ♦

9	3				5	6		8
				4	6			
	7	5		1		2		4
	4		6		2		3	
7					9		6	2
2		9	8	3		1		
8	1		2		3	5		7
		7			1		2	
		2	5	6			8	

M²S Puzzle 19 ♦

1	4		2	7			3	
3								2
			4		8		7	5
	7	6		1		2	9	
				4	9			
4		9			7	6		8
6	1	8	3			5	4	
					4		2	
2			7			3		1

M²S Puzzle 20 ♦

6		8			2			
		3		8			2	6
2	9		7			3		
	7			1			9	
8					9			3
4		9		2			1	8
1	4			7	6			
		7	9				6	2
9		2			8	1	7	

M²S Puzzle 21 ♦

1		5		7		8		9
	8		9		1			
		2		3			7	
5	7		8		3			4
						7		3
	3	9	5		7	6		
6								7
7		3		8	4		2	
		4		6				1

M²S Puzzle 22 ♦

		8						7
7			1		4		2	
	9	4	7			3		1
				1	3		9	4
	2						5	
4	3			2		6		
1		5	2				3	
		7		5		4		2
	6				8	1		

M²S Puzzle 23 ♦

				1		2		
		1					5	3
			2	7			1	
6		8	3			5		7
7				8	4			
	9		7			3		1
1	4		2					
		7					6	2
	6			3	8		7	

M²S Puzzle 24 ♦

6		8	3		2			
7		3	1			9		6
					5		8	
			2	7				9
3	8				1			
			4					
	7				3	2		4
				4				
4		9			7	6		8

	1							
	5					9		6
2			7		5		8	
	4		2	7			3	9
3		7	9		1	4		
9				3				
	7			1	3	2		4
		1		4	9			
4		9				6		8

M²S Puzzle 26 ◆◆

		6		4			3	
			1		6	8		
4	9		3			1		
6		9		3			2	
		8				3		7
	3		6		2			9
		3				2	9	
9	6			2				
		4	5	9		6		

M²S Puzzle 27 ♦♦

1			6		2		8	
2							6	3
	7	9		3	4	1		
			2		7			9
		7	9	1				8
4		2		8				
5	8			6	1			
		1						7
			5			8	1	

M²S Puzzle 28 ♦♦

			2	7			8	9
			9			3		
6	7				8			
8		6		4		9		5
			6			8		
	9		5		3			
5				6	7		9	
7	2			9	5		1	8

M²S Puzzle 29 ♦♦

	3		2	7			8	9
			9					
6	7				8	5	2	
8	1							5
	5		6			8		
					3			6
5	8			6	7	9		
			8		4			
7	2						1	8

M²S Puzzle 30 ♦♦

	3	4			7		1	
			6	4		7	5	
	7				3			4
	4						3	
			9					
2	6			3	8	1	7	
4			7			3		
3		7		8	4	9		6
	1		3				4	

M²S Puzzle 31 ♦♦

	1		3		2		4	7
					4			6
4		2	7			3	8	
	7		8		3	2		
	2	8						3
				2	7	6		8
				7	6		3	
7		3				4		2
2	6		4	3			7	

M²S Puzzle 32 ♦♦

					6	8		
7		3		5				
	6		4		8	1	7	
	3				7		1	
1		8				7		
6	7			1	3		9	4
8		6				5		7
3				8			2	
	9			6	5			

M²S Puzzle 33 ♦♦

	3		5		7	6		8
			6		9		5	
	7						9	4
			2	7		8	3	
7								2
	6	9	4		8		7	
			3	9		5		7
3						9		6
4	9	2	7		5		8	

M²S Puzzle 34 ♦♦

	8					7	6	
	2		7		3		8	
	4		6		8	3		2
6		8	4				2	
						6		9
2		4		7				
	3			4		2	7	
4		2	3					
				6	2			8

M²S Puzzle 35 ♦♦

7	4			1	6	3		2
	2		3			1		4
				9				
	1	6			4		2	
	5		1	2			4	
4		2		7				3
	3		5		1	2		
2		4					5	1
		1	2			4		

M²S Puzzle 36 ♦♦

8	1			4	7	5		
				1			4	8
		2			5	6		1
6	7			3		1		5
	4		1		9	7		
1			6	7				4
5	8				1		9	2
			4		8	3		
7		4						6

M²S Puzzle 37 ♦♦

				2			5	3	
7						6	2		8
2	9			3		5			
3		5		7	6		4	9	
	6				2		3		7
		7		5				1	6
9				8				2	
		2				9	7	6	
5	3				7	2	9		

M²S Puzzle 38 ♦♦

		5	2		4	6		
9	1		7					
2		7			8	5		9
		1		8	5			2
4			1		9	3		
5		3						6
	3			7	6	1	2	
					2			3
6		2	5			9		4

M²S Puzzle 39 ♦♦

	1	8	9				4	7
7				4				6
2			1				8	
	8	5	2			7		
	6		7			4	2	8
		7		1			9	3
				2	1	8	3	
	4		3		7			9
5		1				6		

M²S Puzzle 40 ♦♦

		7	8		6	2	9	
	2		3		7	4		1
		1						
6		8			4	7	2	
7			1		8		4	6
	9			7				
8		9		4	1	6	7	
	6							9
	7		2	6		8	3	

M²S Puzzle 41 ♦♦

					8			4
	2	8		4				3
				2		6		
5	4			7		8		
7		3	1					2
				3			7	
	1	6	2		3			7
3		7		8			2	
			5		7	3		

M²S Puzzle 42 ♦♦

	4	1			2		3	9
		3	1	5		4	6	
	6		8		4	1	7	
9				2	5		1	8
					6			
6			3			2	9	4
4		2		6			8	1
			4	8		9		
8	1						4	7

M²S Puzzle 43 ♦♦

	1		2		7			5
7			9		6	8		
	9	4		8			7	6
5				7			8	
		2	1		9		6	7
	7	6	8	3		5	2	
	8		7	6			9	4
						7		
		7		9	3		1	8

M²S Puzzle 44 ♦♦

9		4			7	6	1	
1	2					7		
			8		3	2	9	
	6	9				1		
			9		1		6	
	4		2					
8		6		9			4	
			1			9		6
		2		6		3		

M²S Puzzle 45 ♦♦

		1		7			3	
	8		9		1	4	6	
	6					1		
6			8		3		9	4
		8	6			7	5	
		4			7		1	
4	9			6				1
3	5				4			6
			3	9			4	

M²S Puzzle 46 ♦♦

	4	5		7		9		8
		7			9		6	
9				3	4	5	7	
	7	6		1		4	9	
			9	4		3		
4		9	7				1	
		8	2	9		7		5
7						6		9
2		4	5	6	7		8	

M²S Puzzle 47 ◆◆

8			3			7		5
				8	4			
4	9		7			1	8	
	3	4						
1				4		3		
	7		8		3	4	9	
5		1						8
7		3	9		1		6	4
			4				7	

M²S Puzzle 48 ◆◆

6			8	1			9	4
1	2				9		5	3
		4						
					2		4	
		7	1				2	6
4		2		6				1
		1	2			8		9
7			9					2
2	6	9		3		1		

M²S Puzzle 49 ♦♦

8		6	2	9		7		5
					1		2	9
4			5		7	1		
		1		7				8
7	8				9	2	6	
		9	8		4	5		1
6	7	5		1			9	2
			9			3		7
			7	2				

M²S Puzzle 50 ♦♦

		2			1		3	8
1			7		3	2		
8		4	2			5	7	
2		3		1	6	7		5
							2	
		7	4		2	1	8	3
3		8			5	4		2
			1	2			5	7
	2	5		3				

M²S Puzzle 51 ♦♦♦

8		6	2					
		2		8			7	
		3			1	2		4
9								
	2	4			3		1	
				3		5		1
	3			7	2	4		9

M²S Puzzle 52 ♦♦♦

								2
	6		2					9
				9	8			
		9		1			4	
2			3					
6						3		
		2			3			
3			9			4		8
	1	6					9	

2		6	1			4		
					8		6	
4				7				1
		2		1				5
6		9				8		
	8		4		2			6
		7				2		4
				6				3
3					4		1	

2			5				8	
		3		8			2	
			2		3			
								8
		1		4		7		
	7					2		4
	4		6		2			
9			8			1		

M²S Puzzle 55 ♦♦♦

		6		9				
			4					6
4		2			7			1
			3		8		9	4
	2			4		7		3
9								
	4			7	2	8		
			1				6	
2				3				

M²S Puzzle 56 ♦♦♦

7			9		1	4		2
				3				
		4			7			
	2					7		3
			8		3			4
4		2	7				8	
3					4			
			3					7

M²S Puzzle 57 ♦♦♦

			7				1	
1						7		
	7			1				4
	4		6		2			
7		3					6	2
				3		1		
		6						7
			4		1			
4		2			7	3		1

M²S Puzzle 58 ♦♦♦

	8				4	7		
	2		7					
		7		1	8		9	
2						8		
		3						
	1		4				2	7
								8
		2	3			9		
8								6

M²S Puzzle 59 ◆◆◆

	8		2		4			
	2					1		
		7		1	8		9	
2				7		8		3
		3						
	1		4				2	7
			9					8
		2	3		7			
8						2		6

M²S Puzzle 60 ◆◆◆

		6	2				3	
					6			
	9		3					1
				6	1			2
								7
	2				3			
	7			3	4			5
		8	1			7		
	3						8	

M²S Puzzle 61 ♦♦♦

		6	2		7		3	
3				1			4	2
	9							
					1	2		4
		1		2		7		
				9				
	7							1
		8	1		9		6	
1		5	6					9

M²S Puzzle 62 ♦♦♦

			7		5		3	
3								2
4	9		3		8	5	6	
		1					2	5
	4	8	1		9			6
						8	4	
1			5		7		9	
		4						
7		5	9		3	6	1	

M²S Puzzle 63 ♦♦♦

			2					
	4				1	3		7
	7			3	8		2	
		6						
			6				4	2
4		2		8	3			
		3		6		2		4
	6				4			3
	2		3					

M²S Puzzle 64 ♦♦♦

				1			9	2
	2	9	3		7	1		
1								5
4		2				8		3
	1					5		
		8		1			7	
2								
		1			9	4		8

M²S Puzzle 65 ◆◆◆

	7					2		
					6			3
				2		6		8
	4		7	2			3	
2	6			3			7	5
8			2					7
		7		8		9		
4								1

M²S Puzzle 66 ◆◆◆

	4			7			3	
3						2	6	
			8		4			
	3		7		5		1	
8		1						
5		6		1		4		2
		4	5		7			3
7				8		6		
	1		2					

M²S Puzzle 67 ♦♦♦

6				4				
		3			6	8		
	9			8				6
						2		
		9	4					3
						6		
				7		4		9
	4				9			
				3		5	2	

M²S Puzzle 68 ♦♦♦

			8				9	
1					9			3
	3					6		
				3	8			5
	8					4		
5			2	7				9
	1				2			
		7	1				2	
4					5		8	

M²S Puzzle 69 ♦♦♦

	4			7	2	8		
			1					2
						1	7	
	7		3			2		
1								
	3			2				8
	9				7		8	
		7			1		2	
8			2					

M²S Puzzle 70 ♦♦♦

					5			
				4		3		7
	7				8		9	
				3	4			
						2		
1	4			7	2			8
	1							
7			4			6		
	9					1		3

M²S Puzzle 71 ♦♦♦

	2							7
							9	
					4			
	8						6	
				7			3	
6			2			7		
				8			2	
	9						8	

M²S Puzzle 72 ♦♦♦

	1		3				4	
3		7				6		9
			7	6			8	
				2				
	2					3		7
			8		3	4		
5				7			3	
		3	9			2		4
2		9						

M²S Puzzle 73 ♦♦♦

	7		8		3	4		2
8			6				5	
		9			7		1	6
	1				2	7		
			1					9
2	9				5			3
1		5	2		6			
		7			1		6	4
9				3		5		

M²S Puzzle 74 ♦♦♦

3		8					9	
9				2	8	3		
							1	
6		2			1			8
			7				6	
8				6				1
					6		4	
								9
		7	4	9		1		

M²S Puzzle 75 ♦♦♦

3		8		7				
9	4				8	3		7
					4		1	
				1		7		5
4		1			7	6	2	
		7						3
	7			4				
1							6	4
	3		2					

M²S Puzzle 76 ♦♦♦

8		6						
				1			4	
	9							6
						2		4
	6			2				3
				3				
							6	
			6		2	4		

M²S Puzzle 77 ♦♦♦♦

4							7	
	6			4				1
							3	
9			8		6			2
	4							
		6		9			8	
2								
		3		6			2	
						3		

M²S Puzzle 78 ♦♦♦♦

						2	7	
3								1
		1						
			8				4	
	4							
				9				3
2						1		7
			9		1	8		
	1							

M²S Puzzle 79 ♦♦♦♦

					7		8	
3								
		6						
							1	
								3
	7				8			
				2				
	8		1			4		
				3			7	

M²S Puzzle 80 ♦♦♦♦

		8	9					
7				1		2		
5						2		
						7		
			7			1		
	4		6		2	8		
							6	
		2		4				

M²S Puzzle 81 ♦♦♦♦

	4				6	8		
					1		6	
2								
	7		8					4
		8						3
				7				
4						3		
		7					2	
8								

M²S Puzzle 82 ♦♦♦♦

						6		
				4		7		
	4						3	
			9					2
					8	7		
8								
		7	1		4		2	
			7					1

M²S Puzzle 83 ♦♦♦♦

	8		2					
					3			1
	4					2		
2			5					
						9		
	1							
						8		
		2						9
				4				

M²S Puzzle 84 ♦♦♦♦

					6			
	2							
			4					5
		8	9					
				8			4	
		4						
				3		9		1
1								

M²S Puzzle 85 ♦♦♦♦

		6						
				8	1			
	9							
5	4		6					
2		9	3				7	
							9	
		8			6			
				8				

M²S Puzzle 86 ♦♦♦♦

		2	5	4				8
1						2		
					9			
			8		6			5
	8				7	6		
							8	
		8	7					2
			2					
		5				8		

♦ 44 ♦

M²S Puzzle 87 ♦♦♦♦

8								1
		7	4					7
				3				
	3					2		
			9					
							1	
	6				6		3	
		3				8		
				9				

M²S Puzzle 88 ♦♦♦♦

7							2	
	1				5			
4			6					
					3			
8					4		1	
		9				8	3	
3					9			

M²S Puzzle 89 ♦♦♦♦

					6			2
	2		3					
1		3						
		2		7				
							4	
8		6						7
				9			3	
								1
		8						

M²S Puzzle 90 ♦♦♦♦

		8					9	
	4			2	8			
								8
6		2						
			7				6	2
2		3						
					7			6
		7	4			3		1

M²S Puzzle 91 ♦♦♦♦

			6					8
	8				9			
							7	
						8		
			9	4				
	7						9	
2			5			1		
				8			2	
	1		2					

M²S Puzzle 92 ♦♦♦♦

		8	7		2		3	
7							4	
				8				
						9		4
		2			1	7		3
	7		4					
				6		4		
1								
	2				5		1	

M²S Puzzle 93 ♦♦♦♦

				1				4
						7		
				7				
			4					
				1			6	
5						8		
						5		
3				4				6
		2	6					1

M²S Puzzle 94 ♦♦♦♦

					2			8
	8					2		
		2	3					1
4								
	2							7
			3					
		4		7		8		
7			4		1		2	9

M²S Puzzle 95 ♦♦♦♦

6								9
			6				4	
	9			8				
				7				
	4						6	
9			4					
	8			6		4		
1					4	3		
		7						

M²S Puzzle 96 ♦♦♦♦

	7		8					4
					9			
9		4					1	
2		9	4					5
	4			7				
		6						
			1		4		2	
		2	7			3		

M²S Puzzle 97 ◆◆◆◆

	7		8					2
		9						6
				2			4	
7						6		
		4	7					
					6			
3	8					2		
9			4		8			

M²S Puzzle 98 ◆◆◆◆

	1			7			9	
		5		3		8		
6				4				8
			7				6	
	3							
2			8					
	8				7			
						1		

M²S Puzzle 99 ♦♦♦♦

	1							2
						3		
7				3				
2			8		6			
						6		
					2			
6	7				1		3	
		9	8					
			6					1

M²S Puzzle 100 ♦♦♦♦

	9							8
7			1					
8			5				7	
		2		8				
								4
	4				6			
3				9			6	7

M²S Puzzle 101 ◆◆◆◆

	1		5				9	4
		7				6		
				4			3	
9		1						
		8						
3					8			
							2	
					4			

M²S Puzzle 102 ◆◆◆◆

			2				7	
6							2	
			6					
2		6					4	
			4	6				
		8	1			9		
						6		
1					6			3
		5						

Puzzles contain less than 3 magic squares

M²S Puzzle 103 ♦

	1		4		7	9		
3		7					4	
			8	3			7	6
6		9		8		5	2	
					9			7
1			7		2		8	9
	8	3				2		4
				4				
7		4	9		3	6		8

M²S Puzzle 104 ♦

1		9		2				7
	7		3			4	8	
8		4			9		2	
				8				5
	1	6		3	7		4	2
3	8				2			
7			8					
	2	8			1	7	5	
				7	4		1	

M²S Puzzle 105 ♦

2		6		3		4		
	5		2		8		6	7
4				7		5	2	
	1	9				8		
7		2		1			3	
	8		4		2	1		6
	6					2		
8		4	9		1		5	
3		5	7		4	6		8

M²S Puzzle 106 ♦

3		7		8			2	
4			7			3		1
	1	6	3		2			
		4				6		8
1	2		6			7		
	7			1	3		9	4
				7			3	
		3	9					2
2		9	4		8	1	7	

8		6		9			4	7
				8		9	2	6
	9	2			5	3		
9		4			7		1	8
			6		9			3
6	7		8	1			9	
	4	1	2		6	8		9
7	8						6	
		9	4		8			5

	4		2	7			3	9
7		3			1	4		2
	6		4		8			
9		4		2		6		
			6					3
	7				3			4
8		6		9	2			7
3				8			2	
		2	7		5	3		1

M²S Puzzle 109 ♦

	3		5	2			1	
						7		3
	7		8		3			4
					1		6	
5		1		7				9
	6		4				7	
8		6			2			
		7		8		9	2	
			7		5	3		1

M²S Puzzle 110 ♦

	4		8		6		9	2
		6	3			1		
3		1		9		7	6	
	1				4		2	7
		3	1		8	6		9
	9			7			1	
	3	9		4			7	
		5		6		4		8
4	6		7		3	9		

M²S Puzzle 111 ♦

	2		3		7			4
7			8				9	
1		3				7		5
			9		4		2	
3			1				4	
	9	2		7		8		3
			5		1		7	
2	6			8		9		1
5	7		2		9		3	

M²S Puzzle 112 ♦

5		6			3	2		4
	2							3
		9		2	7	6		
1				7	6			
3					1			2
	6		4			1		5
		3		8				6
	1					5	4	
		4	7		5			1

M²S Puzzle 113 ◆

		6		4			3	
	5		9				4	
4		2		8		1		
	6		4					3
5	8			6		2		4
		4					1	
	7		8		4	5		1
2	4							7
1		5	6		2		8	

M²S Puzzle 114 ◆

		9		3		5		1
2			1		9			
1	3			7		4		9
		3					9	
7		4		9	3			8
	6		4		8			3
	1		2				3	
		7		1				2
4				8			7	

M²S Puzzle 115 ♦

9		6	3		7	4		1
5						2		
		1		9	2			7
6			9				2	
		3		2	8			
2			6			3	1	8
	3						7	
4		2		8	3			9
1	7					8		

M²S Puzzle 116 ♦

7			8			3	9	
	2		3		7			4
		3			2	7		
3	5					6		9
8			9		4			
		2	6			8		3
5						4		8
2		4	7		3			
	3			4	1			6

M²S Puzzle 117 ♦

3		7		5		4		2
			6			8	3	
9		2			4		7	
	7	6						4
8			9		6		5	
			7			6		8
6				9	3		4	
			4					
2		4		6	7			1

M²S Puzzle 118 ♦

1				7			3	
3		7	1			4		
			8		4		7	
	7	6			8			4
8		1		4			5	
			7			6		8
7			4		1			
6		8					4	7
		4		6	7			1

3		7	9		6			
	1	6		4		9		
	9		3		5		7	
1	3			7		4		9
			1	5			6	
6		9				5		1
7				9			1	
					8	7		3
			7	6	1		9	

	2			4	6			
9		4		2		6		8
6							9	
			6		2	8		9
7				5			6	2
		9	8		4			
			2					
		7		8		9		6
4		2			7		8	

M²S Puzzle 121 ♦

7					4			6
	1					5		
2		4	7	6				1
	7			1		2	9	
8			6		9			3
	3	9				6		
1			2		6			9
	8				1		6	
9		2	4			1	7	

M²S Puzzle 122 ♦

6		8		9				7
		4		6				1
7					4	9		
	7		8					4
8		1		4				
	3				7	6		8
1	4			6			3	
			9		1	4		2
	6	2		3				

M²S Puzzle 123♦

		7		5		4		
	4		2			8	3	
9		2		3				
	7		8		3		9	
								3
	3			2	7	6		
	1		3		2		4	7
		3		8		9	2	
	9	4						1

M²S Puzzle 124 ♦

	1			9		5		7
		3			4			
	9		7					1
1					6		3	
	8		9		1		6	
9		2				1		5
				1			9	
	3		5		7	6		8
8				4			5	

M²S Puzzle 125♦

6				9		5		7
	9		7				8	
		3		8			2	
	7		8		3			4
8		1				7		
	3		5		7			8
1	4							9
			9		1		6	
9		2		3		1		5

M²S Puzzle 126 ♦

8			9		1		6	
1		5		7		8		9
9								
		6		1			9	
8								3
4		9	5	2		6		8
6			3		2		4	
	5				4		2	
		4		6				1

M²S Puzzle 127♦

	1	8			2			
			1			9		6
2			7	6			8	
1			2		6			9
	8			5			6	
9		2				1		
8		1			9	7		
	7			1			9	
		9		2		6	1	

M²S Puzzle 128 ♦

		6		4		9		
		7	9				4	
4				8			7	
6		9	8			5		
	4				9		6	7
		5		7		4		9
	6			2			5	
			7			2		4
7		4		9	3	6		8

M²S Puzzle 129 ♦

	3			7			8	
2		8	1			7		
6				3			2	
	1		2		7		3	
	5					2		
4			3				7	
	6			2		3		
			7					
7		4				8		6

M²S Puzzle 130 ♦

				7	6	4		9
	4	8	9		1		6	7
6								
	1		7	4		9		
	9			8			7	6
		7	6		9	8	4	
	8		1					4
		1			4		5	
7	2		3	9			1	8

M²S Puzzle 131 ♦

			2			4		9
2		8					6	
6			4		8			
		6	7			9		
4	9				3		7	6
		7	6		9		4	
	8		1			2		4
				2		7		3
7		4		9	5			

M²S Puzzle 132 ♦

						6		8
1		8				7		
6	7		8		3			4
	4		2	7			3	
			4					
7		3			1	4	6	
4			7			3		1
		7			4			
	1		3					7

M²S Puzzle 133 ♦

1			3			5		7
		7			4			
	4		7					1
	6		8	1				4
	1						5	
			5		7			8
4			2					
	7				1		6	2
6	2		4			1	7	

M²S Puzzle 134 ♦

	4	1	7			8		9
	8			9	1			
		9	3		8	1		5
9		4						8
1					9			3
	7	5	1		3	2	9	
8			9				4	
		7	8			9		
4					5		8	1

M²S Puzzle 135 ♦

	3				7		1	
			4	6		7		
6	7			8		2	9	
	4	1	7		6	8	3	
				9	1	4		
	6	9		4				
			9	3			4	7
3		7	8			9		
4				7			8	

M²S Puzzle 136 ♦

	3		2		4	7		
2			7		3		8	4
4		7				3	9	
			4		9			
		3					4	9
	2			7		8		3
	8	9			5	2	7	
	4			8			5	
7			9		2			

M²S Puzzle 137 ♦

7	4			8	6		9	
6					7			4
	8		9			7		
		6			4		2	7
			2		8	6		
4	9						1	
9					1	2		6
2		4		7				
	7		6		9	4		

M²S Puzzle 138 ♦

8			4					9
		7	1	9		2	4	
4	9		8				7	1
6		9			4	1	2	
	4	8	5				6	
1	3			6	2	9		4
5	8				1	4	9	2
9		1		4	8			
	2	4	9			8		6

M²S Puzzle 139 ♦

		8			7			9
	7		9	1	6	2		
9	2			8		6		1
8			7		1			2
	1	9		2	8			7
2		7	5	9		8	1	6
7	9							
			1		9	7	6	
3		1	6		2	9	8	

M²S Puzzle 140 ♦

	8			2	4		7	1
				7		2		
2		7		6			3	9
	6	1		3		4		2
4	2				9			7
		3	2	4			1	
	3	4	7		6	1		
1						7		3
6	7		3					4

M²S Puzzle 141 ♦

6	7		5			2		4
	4	8		6				
9	5	3			4		1	
3			6			5	2	1
	1	9			8	3		
			1	3	5		8	
4	2		8			9		5
					7		4	2
8					2			

M²S Puzzle 142 ♦

				1		2		
		6						
		1	4		2		6	
1		8	9		4		2	
				2		9		
9		4	6				1	8
			5		1	6		2
6	4			8				
	1		6	7			3	

M²S Puzzle 143 ♦

6		5			8	2		4
				9			5	3
9	3		2			6		
			7		2	8	3	9
7		3			9			2
	6			8			7	
	1		9			5		7
3						9		
	9		6		7			1

M²S Puzzle 144 ♦

	1	8	9				4	7
7	5				4			6
2			1			8		
	8	5	2			7		
	6		7		5	4		8
		7			1		9	3
			5	1		8	3	
	4		3	7				9
5		1				6		

1		8	2	4		9	3	
				1		8		
	2	4	3		5			
		1						
	8			5		3		
7		6	8	3		5		1
			7			2	9	
	1			2	8		5	3
2		7			3			

9		4			7	6		
	2		4			7		3
			1		3			
2		9		4	8			
	8	3		9		4	6	
5	4		7			8		9
8			9		2			7
				1			2	
4		2				3	8	

M²S Puzzle 147 ♦

5							3	9
		3		9				2
2			3		8	1		
6			1					4
	2	8		6	9		5	
9				5			1	
	9					3		1
3				1	4			
8		6		3		5	4	

M²S Puzzle 148 ♦

			6		2	9	3	
		7			9			
	9	2		3		5	7	
7		6	3			4		
						3		
3		9	7					6
	6		2		3			
						6	2	
9	2		5		7	1		3

M²S Puzzle 149 ♦

8	1			3	2	7		
4		2		7		1		3
		4	2		7		1	
1					9	3		7
	7			8			9	
			7		6			8
	8			9			6	
2			3			5		1

M²S Puzzle 150 ♦

6	7				3			
		8	4			7	5	
	3	4	2		7	6		
8				3	2			7
			8		4		2	
4		2	6	7				1
5	4		7		6	8		
				9	1		6	
2		9	3			1		

M²S Puzzle 151 ♦♦

	8			9	3	7	4	
		7	4				2	
9					7			
4		1	6	7				8
	7		1			2		
6		9					7	1
	6		3		8	4		2
2								
		4					1	6

M²S Puzzle 152 ♦

			4		1		3	
		9		7				4
8		4	6					
2		3			6	7		5
				3			2	
	6	7	9	4				3
3	1			6		4		2
		6	2			3		
7					4			

M²S Puzzle 153 ♦♦

8					7	9		
					6	8		2
4		2	8				7	
	8		6				9	
	6			4				3
7		4				6		
6		9			4		2	
2	4					3	6	
			7		2			9

M²S Puzzle 154 ♦♦

8		4	1	3				2
	7	3	2			1		
				7		8		
		9	8				4	
4	2				7	9		6
		1		9		3		
9		2		8			6	1
	3				1			
1			7	2		5		3

2			3	1				9
		1		2	8	3		7
4				6				
	4	2	1			9	3	
6					7	8		
	8			4			7	
	6	7			3	2		4
8						7		
		5		7	4		1	

2	9		6		7		8	
					1		2	6
6	1		9		3			7
	3	9		7				
					6	7		3
	7		1			2		4
	4			6	2			9
		7				4		
	6		3	8			7	

M²S Puzzle 157 ♦♦

1		6	2		3		4	7
			4					
	4	2						
7			3	1		2		4
								3
3		4	7				1	
4					2	8	3	
			1		9			2
6				3				

M²S Puzzle 158 ♦♦

		1			6		3	
7				9	1		6	2
2		9	3		8			
	3	4		5			1	
		8			9	7		
6					3		9	4
4		2		7			8	
		7	8		4	9		
	1			3			4	

M²S Puzzle 159 ♦♦

	3	4	2	7		6		8
				9	6			
6				8				4
			7	6			3	
7	8				9	4		2
		9		8		1		
8		6		2	3			7
3							2	
		2			7	3		

M²S Puzzle 160 ♦♦

		1			4	7	6	
9					3			
	4		6			3		2
2		4		7	6		1	3
			8		1			
		8				5	2	
					7	9		1
	7			6	2			
			1				7	6

M²S Puzzle 161 ♦♦

	8		9		4		6	
	2			7			8	
		7	1					2
	9				6			3
			2			6		
6		8	4				2	7
1								8
	6							1
		9		1		2		

M²S Puzzle 162 ♦♦

8	1			2				9
	5				6			
				3		6		
		3	7	1		4		
			2					7
7	2		9			8		
6		9	3		4	1	2	
	3		7					4

M²S Puzzle 163 ♦♦

3		1	2		4	7	6	5
	2						8	
5				1				
	9							3
7				2	1			
	1					5	2	7
4	6			8	7			
						4		8
	3		1	4				6

M²⁵S Puzzle 164 ♦♦

3				2	4			5
	2			7		1		
5					8			2
2			7		6	8		3
		3	2					
			3					7
	7							
4		2	8	3		9		1
	3			1	5			6

M²S Puzzle 165 ♦♦

	1		4		7			
		7		9	6	2		
4		2	8			6		1
	8		6		1			2
9	6			4	8	3		
					3		1	6
		9		8		1		5
2		8				7		3
	3	5		6	2		8	4

M²S Puzzle 166 ♦♦

4	7		8					
		9	3		7			
					2		6	
		2	6			8		
					8		4	
1		6			4	5		
3				4	1			
			7		3	9		
				6			3	

M²S Puzzle 167 ♦♦

6	7				3		9	
			4					
9		4	2		7	6	1	
			7					9
	8				1	4		
		9		4				5
							8	
3			8					6
8		6						7

M²S Puzzle 168 ♦♦

	4		7				3	8
		7		1	9		6	
	6		3			5	7	1
	3			7				6
			4			3		7
	7	6			8		9	
	9		6		7	1	8	
7		3	4					9
			2	3		4		

M²S Puzzle 169 ♦♦

		6			7	9		
								2
				8			7	
		3	6		1	2		4
				2				
2	7				3			8
	6		8	3			2	
4		8			9	3		
3				7			8	9

M²S Puzzle 170 ♦♦

6	1		2					
7			6					9
		4		3	7	1		5
8			9		4		1	
	2			7	3		8	
	7		1			3	9	2
5		9	7		2	4		
	4			8				1
1			3	5			7	6

M²S Puzzle 171 ♦♦

	3		7			4		9
		8		9			6	
6	7		3	4				1
8		6	4			9	3	
		7		6			4	2
4			8			1		
5	8						9	4
		1		8				
7			9		5	6		8

M²S Puzzle 172 ♦♦

3		9	7					6
						3		
7			3		8	4		
6		2			4		7	1
			1					
					2	9		8
1		8	2					
5		3			1	6	2	9
				6				

M²S Puzzle 173 ♦♦

4		9				7	2	
			3		7	9		
5					2			
9					1			4
	8	7		6				
			9		8	6		2
6			7					3
		3		2		4		
2			1				6	7

M²S Puzzle 174 ♦♦

	1		3		2	7		
				8			2	
4		2	7			1		
				2			1	6
			6			3		
	7				3	9		
		3	9			2		
				7	6		3	8
2		9				5		

M²S Puzzle 175 ◆◆◆

7		6			3			2
						3		
3			5					6
		8					4	
			1			6		
		2	7					3
	1		2			9		8
8		7			1			
6				3				

M²S Puzzle 176 ◆◆◆

3		8	6				9	
	4				2			7
						8		
		2		1			3	
1								4
		4			6			
2	9				1	7		
				7		6		
		7	4		9			

M²S Puzzle 177 ♦♦♦

	1					4		
		6		2				7
7					4	8		
					6		4	
	8					6		
5				9		1		
		2			1		3	
1			7					4
		4		6			7	

M²S Puzzle 178 ♦♦♦

1				4		9		
					6			
9			3					6
8			7		1			4
						7		
				9				8
7							2	
	2					3		
					2		8	

M²S Puzzle 179 ♦♦♦

	8				3			2
			2			1		
		1			7		3	
	3			6		2		
		2					1	
1				2			8	
	9					7		
			9					
	1			4		5		

M²S Puzzle 180 ♦♦♦

		9				2		
3				4				1
	2							
			8				4	
						6		
1		6	4	9				
								7
		3			1			
6			7				9	

M²S Puzzle 181 ♦♦♦

	4				7	3		1
	3		4	8			2	
		6					4	
3			7		5		1	
2	1							3
				1			9	
4		1	6		2	8		
	7						6	2
				3				

M²S Puzzle 182 ♦♦♦

				3				7
			4					
2		4			6		8	
		6		8				4
	3	9			2		1	8
1						8		
							6	2
	6				3		7	

M²S Puzzle 183 ♦♦♦

	4							9
		3		1		4		
2					3			5
			8		1			
1		8				7		3
9				7	2			
						3		1
3		7		4				
8			3		9			

M²S Puzzle 184 ♦♦♦

3		4	5			6		8
					9			
	6		8					4
		1			6			
						4		
		9	4	3		1	7	
	3					9		6
			7			3		

3				4			6	
		6	7					
						2		3
		4			7			
7								
	1		4			7		
				2		8		
		2		7				
	3		1				7	

	4		8			3		
		6			7			4
3				9		7		
6				3		5		
		3						
2			6				1	
8					1		7	
		2	7					1
					3			

M²S Puzzle 187 ♦♦♦

9		2			6			
							2	
6			4			3		1
	5							
						7		3
		3	6					4
7					1			9
		1	7			4	6	
							7	

M²S Puzzle 188 ♦♦♦

	8			4				7
9			7			4		1
	9							
		8			3	7		
	7			2				
		2		7				9

	2			7		1		
3			4					
		8				5		
7								
	9			5				
8							7	
	6	2	7		8			1
						4		

		1			3	2		
	4			6		7		3
	8			7				1
		9				3		
			1	3			8	
			8					
	6				7			
	3			9		1		6

M²S Puzzle 191 ♦♦♦

7					6			2
		9						
	8			9		7		5
3								
		2	6	7		8		3
		1	2			4		
								1
9	3				1	2		

M²S Puzzle 192 ♦♦♦

3		8	6				9	
				8				
		5			4	6		8
			7					
6					1		3	9
		4		6		1		
2				1				7
		1				9		
	6		4		2			1

M²S Puzzle 193 ♦♦♦♦

1			6					
		7						
				3				1
		9						
2								7
						4		
		4					8	

M²S Puzzle 194 ♦♦♦♦

		8			2			
7				1				
								1
			2					
							6	
					8			
				6				
		9			4	3		

M²S Puzzle 195 ♦♦♦♦

	7						9	
								3
				8				
			7		8			
							4	
4				5				
			1					6

M²S Puzzle 196 ♦♦♦♦

								8
			1			2		
				4				
								6
			3		8		9	
		4			7			
	7							
			2				4	

	7							
						7		
								8
				3				
	8							2
5					6			
			1					
			7				8	

			8					
	2			7				4
		1	4			7	6	5
6					3			7
	9				7	8		
8				1		2		
			7					
	7							8

M²S Puzzle 199 ♦♦♦♦

7								
						3		
					7			6
1							4	
		3		8		6		
							8	
					1	2		4
					8			

M²S Puzzle 200 ♦♦♦♦

						3		
		8						2
7							1	
		2						
								4
	3						7	
			3				2	
				2				

M²S Puzzle 201 ♦♦♦♦

						3		
		8		7				
7							1	
			8		6		4	
								9
				9			8	
		2						8
	3							

M²S Puzzle 202 ♦♦♦♦

9				7				8
		8		3				5
3						6		
	4		7			1		
7								
4						2		
			3					
		1			2			7

M²S Puzzle 203 ♦♦♦♦

	1			7				4
		7		3		6		
9					7			
	7					8		
			6					
							2	
		5		9		3		

M²S Puzzle 204 ♦♦♦♦

		3	2		4		7	
			6				3	
9					2			
	7		8	3				5
	8			2		7		
		5			1			4

		5			2			
							6	
3				1		5		4
		7					8	
6	4							
8				7		2		9
		6						3
					3		2	
	3							

M²S Puzzle 206 ♦♦♦♦

				1				2
	9	6				1		
8					2			5
							2	
	2			7		8		
					1		7	
	4		7	8				
						4		

M²S Puzzle 207 ◆◆◆◆

8					4			
			7			9		
		2						8
		8				5		7
7								
		4					1	
	2			7				
3								

SOLUTIONS

Solutions may vary.

Puzzle 1

```
8 1 6 | 2 4 7 | 9 3 5
3 5 7 | 9 1 6 | 8 4 2
4 9 2 | 3 8 5 | 1 7 6
------+-------+------
6 7 9 | 8 3 4 | 5 2 1
2 4 8 | 1 5 9 | 3 6 7
1 3 5 | 6 7 2 | 4 8 9
------+-------+------
5 8 3 | 7 6 1 | 2 9 4
9 6 1 | 4 2 8 | 7 5 3
7 2 4 | 5 9 3 | 6 1 8
```

Puzzle 2

```
6 7 2 | 1 3 5 | 4 8 9
1 5 9 | 2 4 8 | 3 6 7
8 3 4 | 6 7 9 | 5 2 1
------+-------+------
2 4 7 | 8 1 6 | 9 3 5
9 1 6 | 3 5 7 | 8 4 2
3 8 5 | 4 9 2 | 1 7 6
------+-------+------
7 6 1 | 5 8 3 | 2 9 4
4 2 8 | 9 6 1 | 7 5 3
5 9 3 | 7 2 4 | 6 1 8
```

Puzzle 3

```
2 7 6 | 1 3 5 | 4 8 9
9 5 1 | 2 4 8 | 3 6 7
4 3 8 | 6 7 9 | 5 2 1
------+-------+------
7 4 2 | 8 1 6 | 9 3 5
6 1 9 | 3 5 7 | 8 4 2
5 8 3 | 4 9 2 | 1 7 6
------+-------+------
1 6 7 | 5 8 3 | 2 9 4
8 2 4 | 9 6 1 | 7 5 3
3 9 5 | 7 2 4 | 6 1 8
```

Puzzle 4

```
4 9 2 | 7 6 5 | 3 8 1
3 5 7 | 1 8 4 | 9 2 6
8 1 6 | 3 9 2 | 5 4 7
------+-------+------
9 3 4 | 5 2 7 | 6 1 8
1 2 8 | 6 4 9 | 7 5 3
6 7 5 | 8 1 3 | 2 9 4
------+-------+------
5 4 1 | 2 7 6 | 8 3 9
7 8 3 | 9 5 1 | 4 6 2
2 6 9 | 4 3 8 | 1 7 5
```

Puzzle 5

```
8 1 6 | 3 9 2 | 5 4 7
3 5 7 | 1 8 4 | 9 2 6
4 9 2 | 7 6 5 | 3 8 1
------+-------+------
9 3 4 | 5 2 7 | 6 1 8
1 2 8 | 6 4 9 | 7 5 3
6 7 5 | 8 1 3 | 2 9 4
------+-------+------
5 4 1 | 2 7 6 | 8 3 9
7 8 3 | 9 5 1 | 4 6 2
2 6 9 | 4 3 8 | 1 7 5
```

Puzzle 6

```
5 4 1 | 2 7 6 | 8 3 9
7 8 3 | 9 5 1 | 4 6 2
2 6 9 | 4 3 8 | 1 7 5
------+-------+------
9 3 4 | 5 2 7 | 6 1 8
1 2 8 | 6 4 9 | 7 5 3
6 7 5 | 8 1 3 | 2 9 4
------+-------+------
8 1 6 | 3 9 2 | 5 4 7
3 5 7 | 1 8 4 | 9 2 6
4 9 2 | 7 6 5 | 3 8 1
```

Puzzle 7

```
9 3 4 | 5 2 7 | 6 1 8
1 2 8 | 6 4 9 | 7 5 3
6 7 5 | 8 1 3 | 2 9 4
------+-------+------
5 4 1 | 2 7 6 | 8 3 9
7 8 3 | 9 5 1 | 4 6 2
2 6 9 | 4 3 8 | 1 7 5
------+-------+------
8 1 6 | 3 9 2 | 5 4 7
3 5 7 | 1 8 4 | 9 2 6
4 9 2 | 7 6 5 | 3 8 1
```

Puzzle 8

```
5 4 7 | 8 1 6 | 3 9 2
9 2 6 | 3 5 7 | 1 8 4
3 8 1 | 4 9 2 | 7 6 5
------+-------+------
6 1 8 | 9 3 4 | 5 2 7
7 5 3 | 1 2 8 | 6 4 9
2 9 4 | 6 7 5 | 8 1 3
------+-------+------
8 3 9 | 5 4 1 | 2 7 6
4 6 2 | 7 8 3 | 9 5 1
1 7 5 | 2 6 9 | 4 3 8
```

Puzzle 9

```
7 4 5 | 8 1 6 | 3 9 2
6 2 9 | 3 5 7 | 1 8 4
1 8 3 | 4 9 2 | 7 6 5
------+-------+------
8 1 6 | 9 3 4 | 5 2 7
3 5 7 | 1 2 8 | 6 4 9
4 9 2 | 6 7 5 | 8 1 3
------+-------+------
9 3 8 | 5 4 1 | 2 7 6
2 6 4 | 7 8 3 | 9 5 1
5 7 1 | 2 6 9 | 4 3 8
```

Puzzle 10

5	7	6	8	1	3	2	9	4
8	2	1	6	4	9	7	5	3
4	3	9	5	2	7	6	1	8
1	4	5	2	7	6	8	3	9
3	8	7	9	5	1	4	6	2
9	6	2	4	3	8	1	7	5
6	1	8	3	9	2	5	4	7
7	5	3	1	8	4	9	2	6
2	9	4	7	6	5	3	8	1

Puzzle 11

8	1	6	2	4	7	9	3	5
3	5	7	9	1	6	8	4	2
4	9	2	3	8	5	1	7	6
5	8	3	7	6	1	2	9	4
9	6	1	4	2	8	7	5	3
7	2	4	5	9	3	6	1	8
6	7	9	8	3	4	5	2	1
2	4	8	1	5	9	3	6	7
1	3	5	6	7	2	4	8	9

Puzzle 12

6	7	9	8	3	4	5	2	1
2	4	8	1	5	9	3	6	7
1	3	5	6	7	2	4	8	9
5	8	3	7	6	1	2	9	4
9	6	1	4	2	8	7	5	3
7	2	4	5	9	3	6	1	8
8	1	6	2	4	7	9	3	5
3	5	7	9	1	6	8	4	2
4	9	2	3	8	5	1	7	6

Puzzle 13

5	4	7	8	1	6	2	9	3
9	2	6	3	5	7	4	8	1
3	8	1	4	9	2	5	6	7
6	1	8	9	3	4	7	2	5
7	5	3	1	2	8	9	4	6
2	9	4	6	7	5	3	1	8
8	3	9	5	4	1	6	7	2
4	6	2	7	8	3	1	5	9
1	7	5	2	6	9	8	3	4

Puzzle14

7	4	5	8	1	6	3	9	2
6	2	9	3	5	7	1	8	4
1	8	3	4	9	2	7	6	5
8	1	6	9	3	4	5	2	7
3	5	7	1	2	8	6	4	9
4	9	2	6	7	5	8	1	3
5	7	1	2	6	9	4	3	8
2	6	4	7	8	3	9	5	1
9	3	8	5	4	1	2	7	6

Puzzle 15

1	4	5	6	7	2	8	3	9
3	8	7	1	5	9	4	6	2
9	6	2	8	3	4	1	7	5
5	7	6	3	1	8	2	9	4
8	2	1	9	4	6	7	5	3
4	3	9	7	2	5	6	1	8
6	1	8	2	9	3	5	4	7
7	5	3	4	8	1	9	2	6
2	9	4	5	6	7	3	8	1

Puzzle 16

1	4	5	6	7	2	8	3	9
3	8	7	1	5	9	4	6	2
9	6	2	8	3	4	1	7	5
5	7	6	3	1	8	2	9	4
8	2	1	9	4	6	7	5	3
4	3	9	7	2	5	6	1	8
6	1	8	2	9	3	5	4	7
7	5	3	4	8	1	9	2	6
2	9	4	5	6	7	3	8	1

Puzzle 17

8	1	6	2	4	7	9	3	5
3	5	7	9	1	6	8	4	2
4	9	2	3	8	5	1	7	6
1	3	5	6	7	2	4	8	9
2	4	8	1	5	9	3	6	7
6	7	9	8	3	4	5	2	1
7	2	4	5	9	3	6	1	8
9	6	1	4	2	8	7	5	3
5	8	3	7	6	1	2	9	4

Puzzle 18

9	3	4	7	2	5	6	1	8
1	2	8	9	4	6	7	5	3
6	7	5	3	1	8	2	9	4
5	4	1	6	7	2	8	3	9
7	8	3	1	5	9	4	6	2
2	6	9	8	3	4	1	7	5
8	1	6	2	9	3	5	4	7
3	5	7	4	8	1	9	2	6
4	9	2	5	6	7	3	8	1

Puzzle 19

1	4	5	2	7	6	8	3	9
3	8	7	9	5	1	4	6	2
9	6	2	4	3	8	1	7	5
5	7	6	8	1	3	2	9	4
8	2	1	6	4	9	7	5	3
4	3	9	5	2	7	6	1	8
6	1	8	3	9	2	5	4	7
7	5	3	1	8	4	9	2	6
2	9	4	7	6	5	3	8	1

Puzzle 20

6	1	8	3	9	2	5	4	7
7	5	3	1	8	4	9	2	6
2	9	4	7	6	5	3	8	1
5	7	6	8	1	3	2	9	4
8	2	1	6	4	9	7	5	3
4	3	9	5	2	7	6	1	8
1	4	5	2	7	6	8	3	9
3	8	7	9	5	1	4	6	2
9	6	2	4	3	8	1	7	5

Puzzle 21

1	4	5	2	7	6	8	3	9
3	8	7	9	5	1	4	6	2
9	6	2	4	3	8	1	7	5
5	7	6	8	1	3	2	9	4
8	2	1	6	4	9	7	5	3
4	3	9	5	2	7	6	1	8
6	1	8	3	9	2	5	4	7
7	5	3	1	8	4	9	2	6
2	9	4	7	6	5	3	8	1

Puzzle 22

6	1	8	3	9	2	5	4	7
7	5	3	1	8	4	9	2	6
2	9	4	7	6	5	3	8	1
5	7	6	8	1	3	2	9	4
8	2	1	6	4	9	7	5	3
4	3	9	5	2	7	6	1	8
1	4	5	2	7	6	8	3	9
3	8	7	9	5	1	4	6	2
9	6	2	4	3	8	1	7	5

Puzzle 23

5	7	6	8	1	3	2	9	4
8	2	1	6	4	9	7	5	3
4	3	9	5	2	7	6	1	8
6	1	8	3	9	2	5	4	7
7	5	3	1	8	4	9	2	6
2	9	4	7	6	5	3	8	1
1	4	5	2	7	6	8	3	9
3	8	7	9	5	1	4	6	2
9	6	2	4	3	8	1	7	5

Puzzle 24

6	1	8	3	9	2	5	4	7
7	5	3	1	8	4	9	2	6
2	9	4	7	6	5	3	8	1
1	4	5	2	7	6	8	3	9
3	8	7	9	5	1	4	6	2
9	6	2	4	3	8	1	7	5
5	7	6	8	1	3	2	9	4
8	2	1	6	4	9	7	5	3
4	3	9	5	2	7	6	1	8

Puzzle 25

6	1	8	3	9	2	5	4	7
7	5	3	1	8	4	9	2	6
2	9	4	7	6	5	3	8	1
1	4	5	2	7	6	8	3	9
3	8	7	9	5	1	4	6	2
9	6	2	4	3	8	1	7	5
5	7	6	8	1	3	2	9	4
8	2	1	6	4	9	7	5	3
4	3	9	5	2	7	6	1	8

Puzzle 26

8	1	6	2	4	7	9	3	5
3	5	7	9	1	6	8	4	2
4	9	2	3	8	5	1	7	6
6	7	9	8	3	4	5	2	1
2	4	8	1	5	9	3	6	7
1	3	5	6	7	2	4	8	9
5	8	3	7	6	1	2	9	4
9	6	1	4	2	8	7	5	3
7	2	4	5	9	3	6	1	8

Puzzle 27

1	3	5	6	7	2	9	8	4
2	4	8	1	5	9	7	6	3
6	7	9	8	3	4	1	2	5
8	1	6	2	4	7	5	3	9
3	5	7	9	1	6	2	4	8
4	9	2	3	8	5	6	7	1
5	8	3	7	6	1	4	9	2
9	6	1	4	2	8	3	5	7
7	2	4	5	9	3	8	1	6

Puzzle 28

1	3	5	2	7	6	4	8	9
2	4	8	9	5	1	3	6	7
6	7	9	4	3	8	5	2	1
8	1	6	7	4	2	9	3	5
3	5	7	6	1	9	8	4	2
4	9	2	5	8	3	1	7	6
5	8	3	1	6	7	2	9	4
9	6	1	8	2	4	7	5	3
7	2	4	3	9	5	6	1	8

Puzzle 29

1	3	5	2	7	6	4	8	9
2	4	8	9	5	1	3	6	7
6	7	9	4	3	8	5	2	1
8	1	6	7	4	2	9	3	5
3	5	7	6	1	9	8	4	2
4	9	2	5	8	3	1	7	6
5	8	3	1	6	7	2	9	4
9	6	1	8	2	4	7	5	3
7	2	4	3	9	5	6	1	8

Puzzle 30

9	3	4	5	2	7	6	1	8
1	2	8	6	4	9	7	5	3
6	7	5	8	1	3	2	9	4
5	4	1	2	7	6	8	3	9
7	8	3	9	5	1	4	6	2
2	6	9	4	3	8	1	7	5
4	9	2	7	6	5	3	8	1
3	5	7	1	8	4	9	2	6
8	1	6	3	9	2	5	4	7

Puzzle 31

8	1	6	3	9	2	5	4	7
3	5	7	1	8	4	9	2	6
4	9	2	7	6	5	3	8	1
6	7	5	8	1	3	2	9	4
1	2	8	6	4	9	7	5	3
9	3	4	5	2	7	6	1	8
5	4	1	2	7	6	8	3	9
7	8	3	9	5	1	4	6	2
2	6	9	4	3	8	1	7	5

Puzzle 32

5	4	1	2	7	6	8	3	9
7	8	3	9	5	1	4	6	2
2	6	9	4	3	8	1	7	5
9	3	4	5	2	7	6	1	8
1	2	8	6	4	9	7	5	3
6	7	5	8	1	3	2	9	4
8	1	6	3	9	2	5	4	7
3	5	7	1	8	4	9	2	6
4	9	2	7	6	5	3	8	1

Puzzle 33

9	3	4	5	2	7	6	1	8
1	2	8	6	4	9	7	5	3
6	7	5	8	1	3	2	9	4
5	4	1	2	7	6	8	3	9
7	8	3	9	5	1	4	6	2
2	6	9	4	3	8	1	7	5
8	1	6	3	9	2	5	4	7
3	5	7	1	8	4	9	2	6
4	9	2	7	6	5	3	8	1

Puzzle 34

3	8	1	2	9	4	7	6	5
9	2	6	7	5	3	1	8	4
5	4	7	6	1	8	3	9	2
6	1	8	4	3	9	5	2	7
7	5	3	8	2	1	6	4	9
2	9	4	5	7	6	8	1	3
8	3	9	1	4	5	2	7	6
4	6	2	3	8	7	9	5	1
1	7	5	9	6	2	4	3	8

Puzzle 35

7	4	5	8	1	6	3	9	2
6	2	9	3	5	7	1	8	4
1	8	3	4	9	2	7	6	5
8	1	6	9	3	4	5	2	7
3	5	7	1	2	8	6	4	9
4	9	2	6	7	5	8	1	3
9	3	8	5	4	1	2	7	6
2	6	4	7	8	3	9	5	1
5	7	1	2	6	9	4	3	8

Puzzle 36

8	1	6	2	4	7	5	3	9
3	5	7	9	1	6	2	4	8
4	9	2	3	8	5	6	7	1
6	7	9	8	3	4	1	2	5
2	4	8	1	5	9	7	6	3
1	3	5	6	7	2	9	8	4
5	8	3	7	6	1	4	9	2
9	6	1	4	2	8	3	5	7
7	2	4	5	9	3	8	1	6

Puzzle 37

6	1	8	2	4	7	5	3	9
7	5	3	9	1	6	2	4	8
2	9	4	3	8	5	6	7	1
3	8	5	7	6	1	4	9	2
1	6	9	4	2	8	3	5	7
4	2	7	5	9	3	8	1	6
9	7	6	8	3	4	1	2	5
8	4	2	1	5	9	7	6	3
5	3	1	6	7	2	9	8	4

Puzzle 38

3	8	5	2	9	4	6	7	1
9	1	6	7	5	3	2	4	8
2	4	7	6	1	8	5	3	9
7	6	1	3	8	5	4	9	2
4	2	8	1	6	9	3	5	7
5	9	3	4	2	7	8	1	6
8	3	4	9	7	6	1	2	5
1	5	9	8	4	2	7	6	3
6	7	2	5	3	1	9	8	4

Puzzle 39

6	1	8	9	3	5	2	4	7
7	5	3	8	4	2	9	1	6
2	9	4	1	7	6	3	8	5
3	8	5	2	9	4	7	6	1
1	6	9	7	5	3	4	2	8
4	2	7	6	1	8	5	9	3
9	7	6	5	2	1	8	3	4
8	4	2	3	6	7	1	5	9
5	3	1	4	8	9	6	7	2

Puzzle 40

5	4	7	8	1	6	2	9	3
9	2	6	3	5	7	4	8	1
3	8	1	4	9	2	5	6	7
6	1	8	9	3	4	7	2	5
7	5	3	1	2	8	9	4	6
2	9	4	6	7	5	3	1	8
8	3	9	5	4	1	6	7	2
4	6	2	7	8	3	1	5	9
1	7	5	2	6	9	8	3	4

Puzzle 41

6	7	5	3	1	8	2	9	4
1	2	8	9	4	6	7	5	3
9	3	4	7	2	5	6	1	8
5	4	1	6	7	2	8	3	9
7	8	3	1	5	9	4	6	2
2	6	9	8	3	4	1	7	5
8	1	6	2	9	3	5	4	7
3	5	7	4	8	1	9	2	6
4	9	2	5	6	7	3	8	1

Puzzle 42

5	4	1	6	7	2	8	3	9
7	8	3	1	5	9	4	6	2
2	6	9	8	3	4	1	7	5
9	3	4	7	2	5	6	1	8
1	2	8	9	4	6	7	5	3
6	7	5	3	1	8	2	9	4
4	9	2	5	6	7	3	8	1
3	5	7	4	8	1	9	2	6
8	1	6	2	9	3	5	4	7

Puzzle 43

6	1	8	2	4	7	9	3	5
7	5	3	9	1	6	8	4	2
2	9	4	3	8	5	1	7	6
5	3	1	6	7	2	4	8	9
8	4	2	1	5	9	3	6	7
9	7	6	8	3	4	5	2	1
3	8	5	7	6	1	2	9	4
1	6	9	4	2	8	7	5	3
4	2	7	5	9	3	6	1	8

Puzzle 44

9	3	4	5	2	7	6	1	8
1	2	8	6	4	9	7	5	3
6	7	5	8	1	3	2	9	4
2	6	9	4	3	8	1	7	5
7	8	3	9	5	1	4	6	2
5	4	1	2	7	6	8	3	9
8	1	6	3	9	2	5	4	7
3	5	7	1	8	4	9	2	6
4	9	2	7	6	5	3	8	1

Puzzle 45

5	4	1	2	7	6	8	3	9
7	8	3	9	5	1	4	6	2
2	6	9	4	3	8	1	7	5
6	7	5	8	1	3	2	9	4
1	2	8	6	4	9	7	5	3
9	3	4	5	2	7	6	1	8
4	9	2	7	6	5	3	8	1
3	5	7	1	8	4	9	2	6
8	1	6	3	9	2	5	4	7

Puzzle 46

1 4 5	6 7 2	9 3 8
3 8 7	1 5 9	2 6 4
9 6 2	8 3 4	5 7 1
5 7 6	3 1 8	4 9 2
8 2 1	9 4 6	3 5 7
4 3 9	7 2 5	8 1 6
6 1 8	2 9 3	7 4 5
7 5 3	4 8 1	6 2 9
2 9 4	5 6 7	1 8 3

Puzzle 47

8 1 6	3 9 2	7 4 5
3 5 7	1 8 4	6 2 9
4 9 2	7 6 5	1 8 3
9 3 4	5 2 7	8 1 6
1 2 8	6 4 9	3 5 7
6 7 5	8 1 3	4 9 2
5 4 1	2 7 6	9 3 8
7 8 3	9 5 1	2 6 4
2 6 9	4 3 8	5 7 1

Puzzle 48

6 7 5	8 1 3	2 9 4
1 2 8	6 4 9	7 5 3
9 3 4	5 2 7	6 1 8
8 1 6	3 9 2	5 4 7
3 5 7	1 8 4	9 2 6
4 9 2	7 6 5	3 8 1
5 4 1	2 7 6	8 3 9
7 8 3	9 5 1	4 6 2
2 6 9	4 3 8	1 7 5

Puzzle 49

8 1 6	2 9 3	7 4 5
3 5 7	4 8 1	6 2 9
4 9 2	5 6 7	1 8 3
5 4 1	6 7 2	9 3 8
7 8 3	1 5 9	2 6 4
2 6 9	8 3 4	5 7 1
6 7 5	3 1 8	4 9 2
1 2 8	9 4 6	3 5 7
9 3 4	7 2 5	8 1 6

Puzzle 50

6 7 2	5 4 1	9 3 8
1 5 9	7 8 3	2 6 4
8 3 4	2 6 9	5 7 1
2 9 3	8 1 6	7 4 5
4 8 1	3 5 7	6 2 9
5 6 7	4 9 2	1 8 3
3 1 8	6 7 5	4 9 2
9 4 6	1 2 8	3 5 7
7 2 5	9 3 4	8 1 6

Puzzle 51

8 1 6	2 4 7	9 3 5
3 5 7	9 1 6	8 4 2
4 9 2	3 8 5	1 7 6
5 8 3	7 6 1	2 9 4
9 6 1	4 2 8	7 5 3
7 2 4	5 9 3	6 1 8
6 7 9	8 3 4	5 2 1
2 4 8	1 5 9	3 6 7
1 3 5	6 7 2	4 8 9

Puzzle 52

9 8 4	1 3 5	6 7 2
7 6 3	2 4 8	1 5 9
1 2 5	6 7 9	8 3 4
5 3 9	8 1 6	2 4 7
2 4 8	3 5 7	9 1 6
6 7 1	4 9 2	3 8 5
4 9 2	5 8 3	7 6 1
3 5 7	9 6 1	4 2 8
8 1 6	7 2 4	5 9 3

Puzzle 53

2 7 6	1 3 5	4 8 9
9 5 1	2 4 8	3 6 7
4 3 8	6 7 9	5 2 1
7 4 2	8 1 6	9 3 5
6 1 9	3 5 7	8 4 2
5 8 3	4 9 2	1 7 6
1 6 7	5 8 3	2 9 4
8 2 4	9 6 1	7 5 3
3 9 5	7 2 4	6 1 8

Puzzle 54

2 9 4	5 6 7	3 8 1
7 5 3	4 8 1	9 2 6
6 1 8	2 9 3	5 4 7
4 3 9	7 2 5	6 1 8
8 2 1	9 4 6	7 5 3
5 7 6	3 1 8	2 9 4
1 4 5	6 7 2	8 3 9
3 8 7	1 5 9	4 6 2
9 6 2	8 3 4	1 7 5

Puzzle 55

8	1	6	2	9	3	5	4	7
3	5	7	4	8	1	9	2	6
4	9	2	5	6	7	3	8	1
6	7	5	3	1	8	2	9	4
1	2	8	9	4	6	7	5	3
9	3	4	7	2	5	6	1	8
5	4	1	6	7	2	8	3	9
7	8	3	1	5	9	4	6	2
2	6	9	8	3	4	1	7	5

Puzzle 56

5	4	1	2	7	6	8	3	9
7	8	3	9	5	1	4	6	2
2	6	9	4	3	8	1	7	5
9	3	4	5	2	7	6	1	8
1	2	8	6	4	9	7	5	3
6	7	5	8	1	3	2	9	4
4	9	2	7	6	5	3	8	1
3	5	7	1	8	4	9	2	6
8	1	6	3	9	2	5	4	7

Puzzle 57

9	3	4	7	2	5	6	1	8
1	2	8	9	4	6	7	5	3
6	7	5	3	1	8	2	9	4
5	4	1	6	7	2	8	3	9
7	8	3	1	5	9	4	6	2
2	6	9	8	3	4	1	7	5
8	1	6	2	9	3	5	4	7
3	5	7	4	8	1	9	2	6
4	9	2	5	6	7	3	8	1

Puzzle 58

3	8	1	2	9	4	7	6	5
9	2	6	7	5	3	1	8	4
5	4	7	6	1	8	3	9	2
2	9	4	5	7	6	8	1	3
7	5	3	8	2	1	6	4	9
6	1	8	4	3	9	5	2	7
1	7	5	9	6	2	4	3	8
4	6	2	3	8	7	9	5	1
8	3	9	1	4	5	2	7	6

Puzzle 59

3	8	1	2	9	4	7	6	5
9	2	6	7	5	3	1	8	4
5	4	7	6	1	8	3	9	2
2	9	4	5	7	6	8	1	3
7	5	3	8	2	1	6	4	9
6	1	8	4	3	9	5	2	7
1	7	5	9	6	2	4	3	8
4	6	2	3	8	7	9	5	1
8	3	9	1	4	5	2	7	6

Puzzle 60

8	1	6	2	4	7	5	3	9
3	5	7	9	1	6	2	4	8
4	9	2	3	8	5	6	7	1
5	8	3	7	6	1	4	9	2
9	6	1	4	2	8	3	5	7
7	2	4	5	9	3	8	1	6
6	7	9	8	3	4	1	2	5
2	4	8	1	5	9	7	6	3
1	3	5	6	7	2	9	8	4

Puzzle 61

8	1	6	2	4	7	9	3	5
3	5	7	9	1	6	8	4	2
4	9	2	3	8	5	1	7	6
5	8	3	7	6	1	2	9	4
9	6	1	4	2	8	7	5	3
7	2	4	5	9	3	6	1	8
6	7	9	8	3	4	5	2	1
2	4	8	1	5	9	3	6	7
1	3	5	6	7	2	4	8	9

Puzzle 62

8	1	6	7	2	5	4	3	9
3	5	7	4	9	6	1	8	2
4	9	2	3	1	8	5	6	7
6	7	1	8	3	4	9	2	5
2	4	8	1	5	9	3	7	6
5	3	9	6	7	2	8	4	1
1	6	3	5	8	7	2	9	4
9	8	4	2	6	1	7	5	3
7	2	5	9	4	3	6	1	8

Puzzle 63

1	3	5	2	7	6	4	8	9
2	4	8	9	5	1	3	6	7
6	7	9	4	3	8	5	2	1
8	1	6	7	4	2	9	3	5
3	5	7	6	1	9	8	4	2
4	9	2	5	8	3	1	7	6
5	8	3	1	6	7	2	9	4
9	6	1	8	2	4	7	5	3
7	2	4	3	9	5	6	1	8

Puzzle 64

7	4	5	8	1	6	3	9	2
6	2	9	3	5	7	1	8	4
1	8	3	4	9	2	7	6	5
4	9	2	6	7	5	8	1	3
3	5	7	1	2	8	6	4	9
8	1	6	9	3	4	5	2	7
9	3	8	5	4	1	2	7	6
2	6	4	7	8	3	9	5	1
5	7	1	2	6	9	4	3	8

Puzzle 65

6	7	5	3	1	8	2	9	4
1	2	8	9	4	6	7	5	3
9	3	4	7	2	5	6	1	8
5	4	1	6	7	2	8	3	9
7	8	3	1	5	9	4	6	2
2	6	9	8	3	4	1	7	5
8	1	6	2	9	3	5	4	7
3	5	7	4	8	1	9	2	6
4	9	2	5	6	7	3	8	1

Puzzle 66

1	4	5	6	7	2	9	3	8
3	8	7	1	5	9	2	6	4
9	6	2	8	3	4	5	7	1
4	3	9	7	2	5	8	1	6
8	2	1	9	4	6	3	5	7
5	7	6	3	1	8	4	9	2
2	9	4	5	6	7	1	8	3
7	5	3	4	8	1	6	2	9
6	1	8	2	9	3	7	4	5

Puzzle 67

6	1	8	2	4	7	9	3	5
7	5	3	9	1	6	8	4	2
2	9	4	3	8	5	1	7	6
3	8	5	7	6	1	2	9	4
1	6	9	4	2	8	7	5	3
4	2	7	5	9	3	6	1	8
5	3	1	6	7	2	4	8	9
8	4	2	1	5	9	3	6	7
9	7	6	8	3	4	5	2	1

Puzzle 68

6	7	5	8	1	3	2	9	4
1	2	8	6	4	9	7	5	3
9	3	4	5	2	7	6	1	8
2	6	9	4	3	8	1	7	5
7	8	3	9	5	1	4	6	2
5	4	1	2	7	6	8	3	9
8	1	6	3	9	2	5	4	7
3	5	7	1	8	4	9	2	6
4	9	2	7	6	5	3	8	1

Puzzle 69

5	4	1	6	7	2	8	3	9
7	8	3	1	5	9	4	6	2
2	6	9	8	3	4	1	7	5
6	7	5	3	1	8	2	9	4
1	2	8	9	4	6	7	5	3
9	3	4	7	2	5	6	1	8
4	9	2	5	6	7	3	8	1
3	5	7	4	8	1	9	2	6
8	1	6	2	9	3	5	4	7

Puzzle 70

4	3	9	7	2	5	8	1	6
8	2	1	9	4	6	3	5	7
5	7	6	3	1	8	4	9	2
9	6	2	8	3	4	5	7	1
3	8	7	1	5	9	2	6	4
1	4	5	6	7	2	9	3	8
6	1	8	2	9	3	7	4	5
7	5	3	4	8	1	6	2	9
2	9	4	5	6	7	1	8	3

Puzzle 71

4	3	9	7	2	5	8	1	6
8	2	1	9	4	6	3	5	7
5	7	6	3	1	8	4	9	2
9	6	2	8	3	4	5	7	1
3	8	7	1	5	9	2	6	4
1	4	5	6	7	2	9	3	8
6	1	8	2	9	3	7	4	5
7	5	3	4	8	1	6	2	9
2	9	4	5	6	7	1	8	3

Puzzle 72

8	1	6	3	9	2	7	4	5
3	5	7	1	8	4	6	2	9
4	9	2	7	6	5	1	8	3
9	3	4	5	2	7	8	1	6
1	2	8	6	4	9	3	5	7
6	7	5	8	1	3	4	9	2
5	4	1	2	7	6	9	3	8
7	8	3	9	5	1	2	6	4
2	6	9	4	3	8	5	7	1

Puzzle 73

5	7	6	8	1	3	4	9	2
8	2	1	6	4	9	3	5	7
4	3	9	5	2	7	8	1	6
6	1	8	3	9	2	7	4	5
7	5	3	1	8	4	6	2	9
2	9	4	7	6	5	1	8	3
1	4	5	2	7	6	9	3	8
3	8	7	9	5	1	2	6	4
9	6	2	4	3	8	5	7	1

Puzzle 74

3	1	8	6	7	5	4	9	2
9	4	6	1	2	8	3	5	7
7	2	5	9	3	4	8	1	6
6	7	2	5	4	1	9	3	8
1	5	9	7	8	3	2	6	4
8	3	4	2	6	9	5	7	1
2	9	3	8	1	6	7	4	5
4	8	1	3	5	7	6	2	9
5	6	7	4	9	2	1	8	3

Puzzle 75

3	1	8	6	7	5	4	9	2
9	4	6	1	2	8	3	5	7
7	2	5	9	3	4	8	1	6
2	9	3	8	1	6	7	4	5
4	8	1	3	5	7	6	2	9
5	6	7	4	9	2	1	8	3
6	7	2	5	4	1	9	3	8
1	5	9	7	8	3	2	6	4
8	3	4	2	6	9	5	7	1

Puzzle 76

8	1	6	2	4	7	9	3	5
3	5	7	9	1	6	8	4	2
4	9	2	3	8	5	1	7	6
5	8	3	7	6	1	2	9	4
9	6	1	4	2	8	7	5	3
7	2	4	5	9	3	6	1	8
6	7	9	8	3	4	5	2	1
2	4	8	1	5	9	3	6	7
1	3	5	6	7	2	4	8	9

Puzzle 77

4	8	9	1	3	5	2	7	6
3	6	7	2	4	8	9	5	1
5	2	1	6	7	9	4	3	8
9	3	5	8	1	6	7	4	2
8	4	2	3	5	7	6	1	9
1	7	6	4	9	2	5	8	3
2	9	4	5	8	3	1	6	7
7	5	3	9	6	1	8	2	4
6	1	8	7	2	4	3	9	5

Puzzle 78

4	8	9	1	3	5	2	7	6
3	6	7	2	4	8	9	5	1
5	2	1	6	7	9	4	3	8
9	3	5	8	1	6	7	4	2
8	4	2	3	5	7	6	1	9
1	7	6	4	9	2	5	8	3
2	9	4	5	8	3	1	6	7
7	5	3	9	6	1	8	2	4
6	1	8	7	2	4	3	9	5

Puzzle 79

4	9	2	5	6	7	3	8	1
3	5	7	4	8	1	9	2	6
8	1	6	2	9	3	5	4	7
9	3	4	7	2	5	6	1	8
1	2	8	9	4	6	7	5	3
6	7	5	3	1	8	2	9	4
5	4	1	6	7	2	8	3	9
7	8	3	1	5	9	4	6	2
2	6	9	8	3	4	1	7	5

Puzzle 80

6	1	8	2	9	3	5	4	7
7	5	3	4	8	1	9	2	6
2	9	4	5	6	7	3	8	1
5	7	6	3	1	8	2	9	4
8	2	1	9	4	6	7	5	3
4	3	9	7	2	5	6	1	8
1	4	5	6	7	2	8	3	9
3	8	7	1	5	9	4	6	2
9	6	2	8	3	4	1	7	5

Puzzle 81

5	4	1	2	7	6	8	3	9
7	8	3	9	5	1	4	6	2
2	6	9	4	3	8	1	7	5
6	7	5	8	1	3	2	9	4
1	2	8	6	4	9	7	5	3
9	3	4	5	2	7	6	1	8
4	9	2	7	6	5	3	8	1
3	5	7	1	8	4	9	2	6
8	1	6	3	9	2	5	4	7

Puzzle 82

9	3	4	5	2	7	6	1	8
1	2	8	6	4	9	7	5	3
6	7	5	8	1	3	2	9	4
5	4	1	2	7	6	8	3	9
7	8	3	9	5	1	4	6	2
2	6	9	4	3	8	1	7	5
8	1	6	3	9	2	5	4	7
3	5	7	1	8	4	9	2	6
4	9	2	7	6	5	3	8	1

Puzzle 38

3	8	1	2	9	4	5	6	7
9	2	6	7	5	3	4	8	1
5	4	7	6	1	8	2	9	3
2	9	4	5	7	6	3	1	8
7	5	3	8	2	1	9	4	6
6	1	8	4	3	9	7	2	5
1	7	5	9	6	2	8	3	4
4	6	2	3	8	7	1	5	9
8	3	9	1	4	5	6	7	2

Puzzle 84

5	4	7	8	1	6	3	9	2
9	2	6	3	5	7	1	8	4
3	8	1	4	9	2	7	6	5
6	1	8	9	3	4	5	2	7
7	5	3	1	2	8	6	4	9
2	9	4	6	7	5	8	1	3
8	3	9	5	4	1	2	7	6
4	6	2	7	8	3	9	5	1
1	7	5	2	6	9	4	3	8

Puzzle 85

8	1	6	2	9	3	7	4	5
3	5	7	4	8	1	6	2	9
4	9	2	5	6	7	1	8	3
5	4	1	6	7	2	9	3	8
7	8	3	1	5	9	2	6	4
2	6	9	8	3	4	5	7	1
6	7	5	3	1	8	4	9	2
1	2	8	9	4	6	3	5	7
9	3	4	7	2	5	8	1	6

Puzzle 86

6	7	2	5	4	1	9	3	8
1	5	9	7	8	3	2	6	4
8	3	4	2	6	9	5	7	1
2	9	3	8	1	6	7	4	5
4	8	1	3	5	7	6	2	9
5	6	7	4	9	2	1	8	3
3	1	8	6	7	5	4	9	2
9	4	6	1	2	8	3	5	7
7	2	5	9	3	4	8	1	6

Puzzle 87

8	1	6	2	4	7	9	3	5
3	5	7	9	1	6	8	4	2
4	9	2	3	8	5	1	7	6
5	8	3	7	6	1	2	9	4
9	6	1	4	2	8	7	5	3
7	2	4	5	9	3	6	1	8
6	7	9	8	3	4	5	2	1
2	4	8	1	5	9	3	6	7
1	3	5	6	7	2	4	8	9

Puzzle 88

2	9	4	3	8	7	5	6	1
7	5	3	4	6	1	9	2	8
6	1	8	9	2	5	3	4	7
4	7	5	6	1	8	2	9	3
9	2	1	7	5	3	4	8	6
8	3	6	2	9	4	7	1	5
5	6	9	1	7	2	8	3	4
3	4	2	8	4	9	1	5	9
1	8	7	5	3	6	6	7	2

Puzzle 89

7	4	5	8	1	6	3	9	2
6	2	9	3	5	7	1	8	4
1	8	3	4	9	2	7	6	5
4	9	2	6	7	5	8	1	3
3	5	7	1	2	8	6	4	9
8	1	6	9	3	4	5	2	7
5	7	1	2	6	9	4	3	8
2	6	4	7	8	3	9	5	1
9	3	8	5	4	1	2	7	6

Puzzle 90

3	1	8	6	7	5	2	9	4
9	4	6	1	2	8	7	5	3
7	2	5	9	3	4	6	1	8
6	7	2	5	4	1	8	3	9
1	5	9	7	8	3	4	6	2
8	3	4	2	6	9	1	7	5
2	9	3	8	1	6	5	4	7
4	8	1	3	5	7	9	2	6
5	6	7	4	9	2	3	8	1

Puzzle 91

1 4 5	6 7 2	9 3 8
3 8 7	1 5 9	2 6 4
9 6 2	8 3 4	5 7 1
4 3 9	7 2 5	8 1 6
8 2 1	9 4 6	3 5 7
5 7 6	3 1 8	4 9 2
2 9 4	5 6 7	1 8 3
7 5 3	4 8 1	6 2 9
6 1 8	2 9 3	7 4 5

Puzzle 92

6 1 8	7 4 2	5 3 9
7 5 3	6 1 9	2 4 8
2 9 4	5 8 3	6 7 1
5 3 1	2 7 6	9 8 4
8 4 2	9 5 1	7 6 3
9 7 6	4 3 8	1 2 5
3 8 5	1 6 7	4 9 2
1 6 9	8 2 4	3 5 7
4 2 7	3 9 5	8 1 6

Puzzle 93

6 7 5	8 1 3	2 9 4
1 2 8	6 4 9	7 5 3
9 3 4	5 2 7	6 1 8
2 6 9	4 3 8	1 7 5
7 8 3	9 5 1	4 6 2
5 4 1	2 7 6	8 3 9
8 1 6	3 9 2	5 4 7
3 5 7	1 8 4	9 2 6
4 9 2	7 6 5	3 8 1

Puzzle 94

1 4 5	6 7 2	9 3 8
3 8 7	1 5 9	2 6 4
9 6 2	8 3 4	5 7 1
4 3 9	7 2 5	8 1 6
8 2 1	9 4 6	3 5 7
5 7 6	3 1 8	4 9 2
2 9 4	5 6 7	1 8 3
7 5 3	4 8 1	6 2 9
6 1 8	2 9 3	7 4 5

Puzzle 95

6 1 8	7 4 2	5 3 9
7 5 3	6 1 9	2 4 8
2 9 4	5 8 3	6 7 1
5 3 1	2 7 6	9 8 4
8 4 2	9 5 1	7 6 3
9 7 6	4 3 8	1 2 5
3 8 5	1 6 7	4 9 2
1 6 9	8 2 4	3 5 7
4 2 7	3 9 5	8 1 6

Puzzle 96

6 7 5	8 1 3	2 9 4
1 2 8	6 4 9	7 5 3
9 3 4	5 2 7	6 1 8
2 6 9	4 3 8	1 7 5
7 8 3	9 5 1	4 6 2
5 4 1	2 7 6	8 3 9
8 1 6	3 9 2	5 4 7
3 5 7	1 8 4	9 2 6
4 9 2	7 6 5	3 8 1

Puzzle 97

5 7 6	8 1 3	4 9 2
8 2 1	6 4 9	3 5 7
4 3 9	5 2 7	8 1 6
6 1 8	3 9 2	7 4 5
7 5 3	1 8 4	6 2 9
2 9 4	7 6 5	1 8 3
1 4 5	2 7 6	9 3 8
3 8 7	9 5 1	2 6 4
9 6 2	4 3 8	5 7 1

Puzzle 98

3 1 8	6 7 5	4 9 2
9 4 6	1 2 8	3 5 7
7 2 5	9 3 4	8 1 6
6 7 2	5 4 1	9 3 8
1 5 9	7 8 3	2 6 4
8 3 4	2 6 9	5 7 1
2 9 3	8 1 6	7 4 5
4 8 1	3 5 7	6 2 9
5 6 7	4 9 2	1 8 3

Puzzle 99

3 1 8	6 7 5	4 9 2
9 4 6	1 2 8	3 5 7
7 2 5	9 3 4	8 1 6
2 9 3	8 1 6	7 4 5
4 8 1	3 5 7	6 2 9
5 6 7	4 9 2	1 8 3
6 7 2	5 4 1	9 3 8
1 5 9	7 8 3	2 6 4
8 3 4	2 6 9	5 7 1

Puzzle 100

2	9	4	6	7	5	3	1	8
7	5	3	1	2	8	9	4	6
6	1	8	9	3	4	7	2	5
8	3	9	5	4	1	6	7	2
4	6	2	7	8	3	1	5	9
1	7	5	2	6	9	8	3	4
5	4	7	8	1	6	2	9	3
9	2	6	3	5	7	4	8	1
3	8	1	4	9	2	5	6	7

Puzzle 101

8	1	3	5	7	6	2	9	4
6	4	9	8	2	1	7	5	3
5	2	7	4	3	9	6	1	8
2	7	6	1	4	5	8	3	9
9	5	1	3	8	7	4	6	2
4	3	8	9	6	2	1	7	5
3	9	2	6	1	8	5	4	7
1	8	4	7	5	3	9	2	6
7	6	5	2	9	4	3	8	1

Puzzle 102

8	1	3	2	9	4	5	7	6
6	4	9	7	5	3	8	2	1
5	2	7	6	1	8	4	3	9
2	7	6	8	3	9	1	4	5
9	5	1	4	6	2	3	8	7
4	3	8	1	7	5	9	6	2
3	9	2	5	4	7	6	1	8
1	8	4	9	2	6	7	5	3
7	6	5	3	8	1	2	9	4

Puzzle 103

8	1	6	4	2	7	9	3	5
3	5	7	1	9	6	8	4	2
4	9	2	8	3	5	1	7	6
6	7	9	3	8	4	5	2	1
2	4	8	5	1	9	3	6	7
1	3	5	7	6	2	4	8	9
5	8	3	6	7	1	2	9	4
9	6	1	2	4	8	7	5	3
7	2	4	9	5	3	6	1	8

Puzzle 104

1	5	9	4	2	8	3	6	7
6	7	2	3	1	5	4	8	9
8	3	4	7	6	9	5	2	1
2	4	7	1	8	6	9	3	5
9	1	6	5	3	7	8	4	2
3	8	5	9	4	2	1	7	6
7	6	1	8	5	3	2	9	4
4	2	8	6	9	1	7	5	3
5	9	3	2	7	4	6	1	8

Puzzle 105

2	7	6	1	3	5	4	8	9
9	5	1	2	4	8	3	6	7
4	3	8	6	7	9	5	2	1
6	1	9	3	5	7	8	4	2
7	4	2	8	1	6	9	3	5
5	8	3	4	9	2	1	7	6
1	6	7	5	8	3	2	9	4
8	2	4	9	6	1	7	5	3
3	9	5	7	2	4	6	1	8

Puzzle 106

3	5	7	1	8	4	9	2	6
4	9	2	7	6	5	3	8	1
8	1	6	3	9	2	5	4	7
9	3	4	5	2	7	6	1	8
1	2	8	6	4	9	7	5	3
6	7	5	8	1	3	2	9	4
5	4	1	2	7	6	8	3	9
7	8	3	9	5	1	4	6	2
2	6	9	4	3	8	1	7	5

Puzzle 107

8	1	6	3	9	2	5	4	7
3	5	7	1	8	4	9	2	6
4	9	2	7	6	5	3	8	1
9	3	4	5	2	7	6	1	8
1	2	8	6	4	9	7	5	3
6	7	5	8	1	3	2	9	4
5	4	1	2	7	6	8	3	9
7	8	3	9	5	1	4	6	2
2	6	9	4	3	8	1	7	5

Puzzle 108

5	4	1	2	7	6	8	3	9
7	8	3	9	5	1	4	6	2
2	6	9	4	3	8	1	7	5
9	3	4	5	2	7	6	1	8
1	2	8	6	4	9	7	5	3
6	7	5	8	1	3	2	9	4
8	1	6	3	9	2	5	4	7
3	5	7	1	8	4	9	2	6
4	9	2	7	6	5	3	8	1

Puzzle 109

9	3	4	5	2	7	6	1	8
1	2	8	6	4	9	7	5	3
6	7	5	8	1	3	2	9	4
7	8	3	9	5	1	4	6	2
5	4	1	2	7	6	8	3	9
2	6	9	4	3	8	1	7	5
8	1	6	3	9	2	5	4	7
3	5	7	1	8	4	9	2	6
4	9	2	7	6	5	3	8	1

Puzzle 110

5	4	7	8	1	6	3	9	2
9	2	6	3	5	7	1	8	4
3	8	1	4	9	2	7	6	5
6	1	8	9	3	4	5	2	7
7	5	3	1	2	8	6	4	9
2	9	4	6	7	5	8	1	3
8	3	9	5	4	1	2	7	6
1	7	5	2	6	9	4	3	8
4	6	2	7	8	3	9	5	1

Puzzle 111

6	2	9	3	5	7	1	8	4
7	4	5	8	1	6	3	9	2
1	8	3	4	9	2	7	6	5
8	1	6	9	3	4	5	2	7
3	5	7	1	2	8	6	4	9
4	9	2	6	7	5	8	1	3
9	3	8	5	4	1	2	7	6
2	6	4	7	8	3	9	5	1
5	7	1	2	6	9	4	3	8

Puzzle 112

5	7	6	8	1	3	2	9	4
8	2	1	6	4	9	7	5	3
4	3	9	5	2	7	6	1	8
1	4	5	2	7	6	8	3	9
3	8	7	9	5	1	4	6	2
9	6	2	4	3	8	1	7	5
7	5	3	1	8	4	9	2	6
6	1	8	3	9	2	5	4	7
2	9	4	7	6	5	3	8	1

Puzzle 113

8	1	6	2	4	7	9	3	5
3	5	7	9	1	6	8	4	2
4	9	2	3	8	5	1	7	6
9	6	1	4	2	8	7	5	3
5	8	3	7	6	1	2	9	4
7	2	4	5	9	3	6	1	8
6	7	9	8	3	4	5	2	1
2	4	8	1	5	9	3	6	7
1	3	5	6	7	2	4	8	9

Puzzle 114

6	7	9	8	3	4	5	2	1
2	4	8	1	5	9	3	6	7
1	3	5	6	7	2	4	8	9
5	8	3	7	6	1	2	9	4
7	2	4	5	9	3	6	1	8
9	6	1	4	2	8	7	5	3
8	1	6	2	4	7	9	3	5
3	5	7	9	1	6	8	4	2
4	9	2	3	8	5	1	7	6

Puzzle 115

9	2	6	3	5	7	4	8	1
5	4	7	8	1	6	2	9	3
3	8	1	4	9	2	5	6	7
6	1	8	9	3	4	7	2	5
7	5	3	1	2	8	9	4	6
2	9	4	6	7	5	3	1	8
8	3	9	5	4	1	6	7	2
4	6	2	7	8	3	1	5	9
1	7	5	2	6	9	8	3	4

Puzzle 116

7	4	5	8	1	6	3	9	2
6	2	9	3	5	7	1	8	4
1	8	3	4	9	2	7	6	5
3	5	7	1	2	8	6	4	9
8	1	6	9	3	4	5	2	7
4	9	2	6	7	5	8	1	3
5	7	1	2	6	9	4	3	8
2	6	4	7	8	3	9	5	1
9	3	8	5	4	1	2	7	6

Puzzle 117

3	8	7	1	5	9	4	6	2
1	4	5	6	7	2	8	3	9
9	6	2	8	3	4	1	7	5
5	7	6	3	1	8	2	9	4
8	2	1	9	4	6	7	5	3
4	3	9	7	2	5	6	1	8
6	1	8	2	9	3	5	4	7
7	5	3	4	8	1	9	2	6
2	9	4	5	6	7	3	8	1

Puzzle 118

```
1 4 5 | 6 7 2 | 8 3 9
3 8 7 | 1 5 9 | 4 6 2
9 6 2 | 8 3 4 | 1 7 5
------+-------+------
5 7 6 | 3 1 8 | 2 9 4
8 2 1 | 9 4 6 | 7 5 3
4 3 9 | 7 2 5 | 6 1 8
------+-------+------
7 5 3 | 4 8 1 | 9 2 6
6 1 8 | 2 9 3 | 5 4 7
2 9 4 | 5 6 7 | 3 8 1
```

Puzzle 119

```
3 5 7 | 9 1 6 | 8 4 2
8 1 6 | 2 4 7 | 9 3 5
4 9 2 | 3 8 5 | 1 7 6
------+-------+------
1 3 5 | 6 7 2 | 4 8 9
2 4 8 | 1 5 9 | 3 6 7
6 7 9 | 8 3 4 | 5 2 1
------+-------+------
7 2 4 | 5 9 3 | 6 1 8
9 6 1 | 4 2 8 | 7 5 3
5 8 3 | 7 6 1 | 2 9 4
```

Puzzle 120

```
1 2 8 | 9 4 6 | 7 5 3
9 3 4 | 7 2 5 | 6 1 8
6 7 5 | 3 1 8 | 2 9 4
------+-------+------
5 4 1 | 6 7 2 | 8 3 9
7 8 3 | 1 5 9 | 4 6 2
2 6 9 | 8 3 4 | 1 7 5
------+-------+------
8 1 6 | 2 9 3 | 5 4 7
3 5 7 | 4 8 1 | 9 2 6
4 9 2 | 5 6 7 | 3 8 1
```

Puzzle 121

```
7 5 3 | 1 8 4 | 9 2 6
6 1 8 | 3 9 2 | 5 4 7
2 9 4 | 7 6 5 | 3 8 1
------+-------+------
5 7 6 | 8 1 3 | 2 9 4
8 2 1 | 6 4 9 | 7 5 3
4 3 9 | 5 2 7 | 6 1 8
------+-------+------
1 4 5 | 2 7 6 | 8 3 9
3 8 7 | 9 5 1 | 4 6 2
9 6 2 | 4 3 8 | 1 7 5
```

Puzzle 122

```
6 1 8 | 3 9 2 | 5 4 7
2 9 4 | 7 6 5 | 3 8 1
7 5 3 | 1 8 4 | 9 2 6
------+-------+------
5 7 6 | 8 1 3 | 2 9 4
8 2 1 | 6 4 9 | 7 5 3
4 3 9 | 5 2 7 | 6 1 8
------+-------+------
1 4 5 | 2 7 6 | 8 3 9
3 8 7 | 9 5 1 | 4 6 2
9 6 2 | 4 3 8 | 1 7 5
```

Puzzle 123

```
3 8 7 | 9 5 1 | 4 6 2
1 4 5 | 2 7 6 | 8 3 9
9 6 2 | 4 3 8 | 1 7 5
------+-------+------
5 7 6 | 8 1 3 | 2 9 4
8 2 1 | 6 4 9 | 7 5 3
4 3 9 | 5 2 7 | 6 1 8
------+-------+------
6 1 8 | 3 9 2 | 5 4 7
7 5 3 | 1 8 4 | 9 2 6
2 9 4 | 7 6 5 | 3 8 1
```

Puzzle 124

```
6 1 8 | 3 9 2 | 5 4 7
7 5 3 | 1 8 4 | 9 2 6
2 9 4 | 7 6 5 | 3 8 1
------+-------+------
1 4 5 | 2 7 6 | 8 3 9
3 8 7 | 9 5 1 | 4 6 2
9 6 2 | 4 3 8 | 1 7 5
------+-------+------
5 7 6 | 8 1 3 | 2 9 4
4 3 9 | 5 2 7 | 6 1 8
8 2 1 | 6 4 9 | 7 5 3
```

Puzzle 125

```
6 1 8 | 3 9 2 | 5 4 7
2 9 4 | 7 6 5 | 3 8 1
7 5 3 | 1 8 4 | 9 2 6
------+-------+------
5 7 6 | 8 1 3 | 2 9 4
8 2 1 | 6 4 9 | 7 5 3
4 3 9 | 5 2 7 | 6 1 8
------+-------+------
1 4 5 | 2 7 6 | 8 3 9
3 8 7 | 9 5 1 | 4 6 2
9 6 2 | 4 3 8 | 1 7 5
```

Puzzle 126

```
3 8 7 | 9 5 1 | 4 6 2
1 4 5 | 2 7 6 | 8 3 9
9 6 2 | 4 3 8 | 1 7 5
------+-------+------
5 7 6 | 8 1 3 | 2 9 4
8 2 1 | 6 4 9 | 7 5 3
4 3 9 | 5 2 7 | 6 1 8
------+-------+------
6 1 8 | 3 9 2 | 5 4 7
7 5 3 | 1 8 4 | 9 2 6
2 9 4 | 7 6 5 | 3 8 1
```

Puzzle 127

6	1	8	3	9	2	5	4	7
7	5	3	1	8	4	9	2	6
2	9	4	7	6	5	3	8	1
1	4	5	2	7	6	8	3	9
3	8	7	9	5	1	4	6	2
9	6	2	4	3	8	1	7	5
8	2	1	6	4	9	7	5	3
5	7	6	8	1	3	2	9	4
4	3	9	5	2	7	6	1	8

Puzzle 128

8	1	6	2	4	7	9	3	5
3	5	7	9	1	6	8	4	2
4	9	2	3	8	5	1	7	6
6	7	9	8	3	4	5	2	1
2	4	8	1	5	9	3	6	7
1	3	5	6	7	2	4	8	9
9	6	1	4	2	8	7	5	3
5	8	3	7	6	1	2	9	4
7	2	4	5	9	3	6	1	8

Puzzle 129

1	3	5	6	7	2	9	8	4
2	4	8	1	5	9	7	6	3
6	7	9	8	3	4	1	2	5
8	1	6	2	4	7	5	3	9
3	5	7	9	1	6	2	4	8
4	9	2	3	8	5	6	7	1
9	6	1	4	2	8	3	5	7
5	8	3	7	6	1	4	9	2
7	2	4	5	9	3	8	1	6

Puzzle 130

1	3	5	2	7	6	4	8	9
2	4	8	9	5	1	3	6	7
6	7	9	4	3	8	5	2	1
8	1	6	7	4	2	9	3	5
4	9	2	5	8	3	1	7	6
3	5	7	6	1	9	8	4	2
5	8	3	1	6	7	2	9	4
9	6	1	8	2	4	7	5	3
7	2	4	3	9	5	6	1	8

Puzzle 131

1	3	5	2	7	6	4	8	9
2	4	8	9	5	1	3	6	7
6	7	9	4	3	8	5	2	1
8	1	6	7	4	2	9	3	5
4	9	2	5	8	3	1	7	6
3	5	7	6	1	9	8	4	2
5	8	3	1	6	7	2	9	4
9	6	1	8	2	4	7	5	3
7	2	4	3	9	5	6	1	8

Puzzle 132

9	3	4	5	2	7	6	1	8
1	2	8	6	4	9	7	5	3
6	7	5	8	1	3	2	9	4
5	4	1	2	7	6	8	3	9
2	6	9	4	3	8	1	7	5
7	8	3	9	5	1	4	6	2
4	9	2	7	6	5	3	8	1
3	5	7	1	8	4	9	2	6
8	1	6	3	9	2	5	4	7

Puzzle 133

1	8	6	3	9	2	5	4	7
5	3	7	1	8	4	9	2	6
9	4	2	7	6	5	3	8	1
7	6	5	8	1	3	2	9	4
2	1	8	6	4	9	7	5	3
3	9	4	5	2	7	6	1	8
4	5	1	2	7	6	8	3	9
8	7	3	9	5	1	4	6	2
6	2	9	4	3	8	1	7	5

Puzzle 134

5	4	1	7	2	6	8	3	9
7	8	3	5	9	1	4	6	2
2	6	9	3	4	8	1	7	5
9	3	4	2	5	7	6	1	8
1	2	8	4	6	9	7	5	3
6	7	5	1	8	3	2	9	4
8	1	6	9	3	2	5	4	7
3	5	7	8	1	4	9	2	6
4	9	2	6	7	5	3	8	1

Puzzle 135

9	3	4	2	5	7	6	1	8
1	2	8	4	6	9	7	5	3
6	7	5	1	8	3	2	9	4
5	4	1	7	2	6	8	3	9
7	8	3	5	9	1	4	6	2
2	6	9	3	4	8	1	7	5
8	1	6	9	3	2	5	4	7
3	5	7	8	1	4	9	2	6
4	9	2	6	7	5	3	8	1

Puzzle 136

8	3	1	2	9	4	7	6	5
2	9	6	7	5	3	1	8	4
4	5	7	6	1	8	3	9	2
1	6	8	4	3	9	5	2	7
5	7	3	8	2	1	6	4	9
9	2	4	5	7	6	8	1	3
3	8	9	1	4	5	2	7	6
6	4	2	3	8	7	9	5	1
7	1	5	9	6	2	4	3	8

Puzzle 137

7	4	5	1	8	6	3	9	2
6	2	9	5	3	7	1	8	4
1	8	3	9	4	2	7	6	5
8	1	6	3	9	4	5	2	7
3	5	7	2	1	8	6	4	9
4	9	2	7	6	5	8	1	3
9	3	8	4	5	1	2	7	6
2	6	4	8	7	3	9	5	1
5	7	1	6	2	9	4	3	8

Puzzle 138

8	1	6	4	2	7	5	3	9
3	5	7	1	9	6	2	4	8
4	9	2	8	3	5	6	7	1
6	7	9	3	8	4	1	2	5
2	4	8	5	1	9	7	6	3
1	3	5	7	6	2	9	8	4
5	8	3	6	7	1	4	9	2
9	6	1	2	4	8	3	5	7
7	2	4	9	5	3	8	1	6

Puzzle 139

1	6	8	2	4	7	5	3	9
5	7	3	9	1	6	2	4	8
9	2	4	3	8	5	6	7	1
8	3	5	7	6	1	4	9	2
6	1	9	4	2	8	3	5	7
2	4	7	5	9	3	8	1	6
7	9	6	8	3	4	1	2	5
4	8	2	1	5	9	7	6	3
3	5	1	6	7	2	9	8	4

Puzzle 140

3	8	5	9	2	4	6	7	1
9	1	6	5	7	3	2	4	8
2	4	7	1	6	8	5	3	9
7	6	1	8	3	5	4	9	2
4	2	8	6	1	9	3	5	7
5	9	3	2	4	7	8	1	6
8	3	4	7	9	6	1	2	5
1	5	9	4	8	2	7	6	3
6	7	2	3	5	1	9	8	4

Puzzle 141

6	7	1	5	8	3	2	9	4
2	4	8	9	6	1	7	5	3
9	5	3	7	2	4	6	1	8
3	8	4	6	7	9	5	2	1
5	1	9	2	4	8	3	6	7
7	6	2	1	3	5	4	8	9
4	2	7	8	1	6	9	3	5
1	9	6	3	5	7	8	4	2
8	3	5	4	9	2	1	7	6

Puzzle 142

4	5	7	8	1	6	2	9	3
2	9	6	3	5	7	4	8	1
8	3	1	4	9	2	5	6	7
1	6	8	9	3	4	7	2	5
5	7	3	1	2	8	9	4	6
9	2	4	6	7	5	3	1	8
3	8	9	5	4	1	6	7	2
6	4	2	7	8	3	1	5	9
7	1	5	2	6	9	8	3	4

Puzzle 143

6	7	5	1	3	8	2	9	4
1	2	8	4	9	6	7	5	3
9	3	4	2	7	5	6	1	8
5	4	1	7	6	2	8	3	9
7	8	3	5	1	9	4	6	2
2	6	9	3	8	4	1	7	5
8	1	6	9	2	3	5	4	7
3	5	7	8	4	1	9	2	6
4	9	2	6	5	7	3	8	1

Puzzle 144

6	1	8	9	5	3	2	4	7
7	5	3	8	2	4	9	1	6
2	9	4	1	6	7	3	8	5
3	8	5	2	4	9	7	6	1
1	6	9	7	3	5	4	2	8
4	2	7	6	8	1	5	9	3
9	7	6	5	1	2	8	3	4
8	4	2	3	7	6	1	5	9
5	3	1	4	9	8	6	7	2

Puzzle 145

1 6 8	2 4 7	9 3 5
5 7 3	9 1 6	8 4 2
9 2 4	3 8 5	1 7 6
3 5 1	6 7 2	4 8 9
4 8 2	1 5 9	3 6 7
7 9 6	8 3 4	5 2 1
8 3 5	7 6 1	2 9 4
6 1 9	4 2 8	7 5 3
2 4 7	5 9 3	6 1 8

Puzzle 146

9 3 4	2 5 7	6 1 8
1 2 8	4 6 9	7 5 3
6 7 5	1 8 3	2 9 4
2 6 9	3 4 8	1 7 5
7 8 3	5 9 1	4 6 2
5 4 1	7 2 6	8 3 9
8 1 6	9 3 2	5 4 7
3 5 7	8 1 4	9 2 6
4 9 2	6 7 5	3 8 1

Puzzle 147

5 4 1	7 2 6	8 3 9
7 8 3	5 9 1	4 6 2
2 6 9	3 4 8	1 7 5
6 7 5	1 8 3	2 9 4
1 2 8	4 6 9	7 5 3
9 3 4	2 5 7	6 1 8
4 9 2	6 7 5	3 8 1
3 5 7	8 1 4	9 2 6
8 1 6	9 3 2	5 4 7

Puzzle 148

4 1 5	6 7 2	9 3 8
8 3 7	1 5 9	2 6 4
6 9 2	8 3 4	5 7 1
7 5 6	3 1 8	4 9 2
2 8 1	9 4 6	3 5 7
3 4 9	7 2 5	8 1 6
1 6 8	2 9 3	7 4 5
5 7 3	4 8 1	6 2 9
9 2 4	5 6 7	1 8 3

Puzzle 149

8 1 6	9 3 2	7 4 5
3 5 7	8 1 4	6 2 9
4 9 2	6 7 5	1 8 3
9 3 4	2 5 7	8 1 6
1 2 8	4 6 9	3 5 7
6 7 5	1 8 3	4 9 2
5 4 1	7 2 6	9 3 8
7 8 3	5 9 1	2 6 4
2 6 9	3 4 8	5 7 1

Puzzle 150

6 7 5	1 8 3	2 9 4
1 2 8	4 6 9	7 5 3
9 3 4	2 5 7	6 1 8
8 1 6	9 3 2	5 4 7
3 5 7	8 1 4	9 2 6
4 9 2	6 7 5	3 8 1
5 4 1	7 2 6	8 3 9
7 8 3	5 9 1	4 6 2
2 6 9	3 4 8	1 7 5

Puzzle 151

1 8 6	2 9 3	7 4 5
5 3 7	4 8 1	6 2 9
9 4 2	5 6 7	1 8 3
4 5 1	6 7 2	9 3 8
8 7 3	1 5 9	2 6 4
6 2 9	8 3 4	5 7 1
7 6 5	3 1 8	4 9 2
2 1 8	9 4 6	3 5 7
3 9 4	7 2 5	8 1 6

Puzzle 152

6 7 2	4 5 1	9 3 8
1 5 9	8 7 3	2 6 4
8 3 4	6 2 9	5 7 1
2 9 3	1 8 6	7 4 5
4 8 1	5 3 7	6 2 9
5 6 7	9 4 2	1 8 3
3 1 8	7 6 5	4 9 2
9 4 6	2 1 8	3 5 7
7 2 5	3 9 4	8 1 6

Puzzle 153

8 1 6	4 2 7	9 3 5
3 5 7	1 9 6	8 4 2
4 9 2	8 3 5	1 7 6
5 8 3	6 7 1	2 9 4
9 6 1	2 4 8	7 5 3
7 2 4	9 5 3	6 1 8
6 7 9	3 8 4	5 2 1
2 4 8	5 1 9	3 6 7
1 3 5	7 6 2	4 8 9

Puzzle 154

8	9	4	1	3	5	6	7	2
6	7	3	2	4	8	1	5	9
2	1	5	6	7	9	8	3	4
3	5	9	8	1	6	2	4	7
4	2	8	3	5	7	9	1	6
7	6	1	4	9	2	3	8	5
9	4	2	5	8	3	7	6	1
5	3	7	9	6	1	4	2	8
1	8	6	7	2	4	5	9	3

Puzzle 155

2	7	6	3	1	5	4	8	9
9	5	1	4	2	8	3	6	7
4	3	8	7	6	9	5	2	1
7	4	2	1	8	6	9	3	5
6	1	9	5	3	7	8	4	2
5	8	3	9	4	2	1	7	6
1	6	7	8	5	3	2	9	4
8	2	4	6	9	1	7	5	3
3	9	5	2	7	4	6	1	8

Puzzle 156

2	9	4	6	5	7	3	8	1
7	5	3	8	4	1	9	2	6
6	1	8	9	2	3	5	4	7
4	3	9	2	7	5	6	1	8
8	2	1	4	9	6	7	5	3
5	7	6	1	3	8	2	9	4
1	4	5	7	6	2	8	3	9
3	8	7	5	1	9	4	6	2
9	6	2	3	8	4	1	7	5

Puzzle 157

1	8	6	2	9	3	5	4	7
5	3	7	4	8	1	9	2	6
9	4	2	5	6	7	3	8	1
7	6	5	3	1	8	2	9	4
2	1	8	9	4	6	7	5	3
3	9	4	7	2	5	6	1	8
4	5	1	6	7	2	8	3	9
8	7	3	1	5	9	4	6	2
6	2	9	8	3	4	1	7	5

Puzzle 158

5	4	1	7	2	6	8	3	9
7	8	3	5	9	1	4	6	2
2	6	9	3	4	8	1	7	5
9	3	4	2	5	7	6	1	8
1	2	8	4	6	9	7	5	3
6	7	5	1	8	3	2	9	4
4	9	2	6	7	5	3	8	1
3	5	7	8	1	4	9	2	6
8	1	6	9	3	2	5	4	7

Puzzle 159

9	3	4	2	7	5	6	1	8
1	2	8	4	9	6	7	5	3
6	7	5	1	3	8	2	9	4
5	4	1	7	6	2	8	3	9
7	8	3	5	1	9	4	6	2
2	6	9	3	8	4	1	7	5
8	1	6	9	2	3	5	4	7
3	5	7	8	4	1	9	2	6
4	9	2	6	5	7	3	8	1

Puzzle 160

3	8	1	2	9	4	7	6	5
9	2	6	7	5	3	1	8	4
5	4	7	6	1	8	3	9	2
2	9	4	5	7	6	8	1	3
7	5	3	8	2	1	6	4	9
6	1	8	4	3	9	5	2	7
4	6	2	3	8	7	9	5	1
1	7	5	9	6	2	4	3	8
8	3	9	1	4	5	2	7	6

Puzzle 161

3	8	1	9	2	4	7	6	5
9	2	6	5	7	3	1	8	4
5	4	7	1	6	8	3	9	2
2	9	4	7	5	6	8	1	3
7	5	3	2	8	1	6	4	9
6	1	8	3	4	9	5	2	7
1	7	5	6	9	2	4	3	8
4	6	2	8	3	7	9	5	1
8	3	9	4	1	5	2	7	6

Puzzle 162

8	1	6	4	2	7	5	3	9
3	5	7	1	9	6	2	4	8
4	9	2	8	3	5	6	7	1
5	8	3	6	7	1	4	9	2
9	6	1	2	4	8	3	5	7
7	2	4	9	5	3	8	1	6
6	7	9	3	8	4	1	2	5
2	4	8	5	1	9	7	6	3
1	3	5	7	6	2	9	8	4

Puzzle 163

```
3 8 1 | 2 9 4 | 7 6 5
9 2 6 | 7 5 3 | 1 8 4
5 4 7 | 6 1 8 | 3 9 2
------+-------+------
2 9 4 | 5 7 6 | 8 1 3
7 5 3 | 8 2 1 | 6 4 9
6 1 8 | 4 3 9 | 5 2 7
------+-------+------
4 6 2 | 3 8 7 | 9 5 1
1 7 5 | 9 6 2 | 4 3 8
8 3 9 | 1 4 5 | 2 7 6
```

Puzzle 164

```
3 8 1 | 9 2 4 | 7 6 5
9 2 6 | 5 7 3 | 1 8 4
5 4 7 | 1 6 8 | 3 9 2
------+-------+------
2 9 4 | 7 5 6 | 8 1 3
7 5 3 | 2 8 1 | 6 4 9
6 1 8 | 3 4 9 | 5 2 7
------+-------+------
1 7 5 | 6 9 2 | 4 3 8
4 6 2 | 8 3 7 | 9 5 1
8 3 9 | 4 1 5 | 2 7 6
```

Puzzle 165

```
8 1 6 | 4 2 7 | 5 3 9
3 5 7 | 1 9 6 | 2 4 8
4 9 2 | 8 3 5 | 6 7 1
------+-------+------
5 8 3 | 6 7 1 | 4 9 2
9 6 1 | 2 4 8 | 3 5 7
7 2 4 | 9 5 3 | 8 1 6
------+-------+------
6 7 9 | 3 8 4 | 1 2 5
2 4 8 | 5 1 9 | 7 6 3
1 3 5 | 7 6 2 | 9 8 4
```

Puzzle 166

```
4 7 5 | 8 1 6 | 3 9 2
2 6 9 | 3 5 7 | 1 8 4
8 1 3 | 4 9 2 | 7 6 5
------+-------+------
9 4 2 | 6 7 5 | 8 1 3
5 3 7 | 1 2 8 | 6 4 9
1 8 6 | 9 3 4 | 5 2 7
------+-------+------
3 9 8 | 5 4 1 | 2 7 6
6 2 4 | 7 8 3 | 9 5 1
7 5 1 | 2 6 9 | 4 3 8
```

Puzzle 167

```
6 7 5 | 1 8 3 | 2 9 4
1 2 8 | 4 6 9 | 7 5 3
9 3 4 | 2 5 7 | 6 1 8
------+-------+------
5 4 1 | 7 2 6 | 8 3 9
7 8 3 | 5 9 1 | 4 6 2
2 6 9 | 3 4 8 | 1 7 5
------+-------+------
4 9 2 | 6 5 7 | 3 8 1
3 5 7 | 8 1 4 | 9 2 6
8 1 6 | 9 2 3 | 5 4 7
```

Puzzle 168

```
1 4 5 | 7 6 2 | 9 3 8
3 8 7 | 5 1 9 | 2 6 4
9 6 2 | 3 8 4 | 5 7 1
------+-------+------
4 3 9 | 2 7 5 | 8 1 6
8 2 1 | 4 9 6 | 3 5 7
5 7 6 | 1 3 8 | 4 9 2
------+-------+------
2 9 4 | 6 5 7 | 1 8 3
7 5 3 | 8 4 1 | 6 2 9
6 1 8 | 9 2 3 | 7 4 5
```

Puzzle 169

```
1 8 6 | 2 4 7 | 9 3 5
5 3 7 | 9 1 6 | 8 4 2
9 4 2 | 3 8 5 | 1 7 6
------+-------+------
8 5 3 | 7 6 1 | 2 9 4
6 9 1 | 4 2 8 | 7 5 3
2 7 4 | 5 9 3 | 6 1 8
------+-------+------
7 6 9 | 8 3 4 | 5 2 1
4 2 8 | 1 5 9 | 3 6 7
3 1 5 | 6 7 2 | 4 8 9
```

Puzzle 170

```
6 1 8 | 2 9 5 | 7 4 3
7 5 3 | 6 4 1 | 8 2 9
2 9 4 | 8 3 7 | 1 6 5
------+-------+------
8 3 6 | 9 2 4 | 5 1 7
9 2 1 | 5 7 3 | 6 8 4
4 7 5 | 1 6 8 | 3 9 2
------+-------+------
5 6 9 | 7 1 2 | 4 3 8
3 4 2 | 4 8 9 | 9 5 1
1 8 7 | 3 5 6 | 2 7 6
```

Puzzle 171

```
1 3 5 | 7 2 6 | 4 8 9
2 4 8 | 5 9 1 | 3 6 7
6 7 9 | 3 4 8 | 5 2 1
------+-------+------
8 1 6 | 4 7 2 | 9 3 5
3 5 7 | 1 6 9 | 8 4 2
4 9 2 | 8 5 3 | 1 7 6
------+-------+------
5 8 3 | 6 1 7 | 2 9 4
9 6 1 | 2 8 4 | 7 5 3
7 2 4 | 9 3 5 | 6 1 8
```

Puzzle 172

3	4	9	7	2	5	8	1	6
2	8	1	9	4	6	3	5	7
7	5	6	3	1	8	4	9	2
6	9	2	8	3	4	5	7	1
8	3	7	1	5	9	2	6	4
4	1	5	6	7	2	9	3	8
1	6	8	2	9	3	7	4	5
5	7	3	4	8	1	6	2	9
9	2	4	5	6	7	1	8	3

Puzzle 173

4	3	9	8	1	6	7	2	5
8	2	1	3	5	7	9	4	6
5	7	6	4	9	2	3	1	8
9	6	2	5	7	1	8	3	4
3	8	7	2	6	4	1	5	9
1	4	5	9	3	8	6	7	2
6	1	8	7	4	5	2	9	3
7	5	3	6	2	9	4	8	1
2	9	4	1	8	3	5	6	7

Puzzle 174

8	1	6	3	9	2	7	4	5
3	5	7	1	8	4	6	2	9
4	9	2	7	6	5	1	8	3
9	3	4	5	2	7	8	1	6
1	2	8	6	4	9	3	5	7
6	7	5	8	1	3	4	9	2
7	8	3	9	5	1	2	6	4
5	4	1	2	7	6	9	3	8
2	6	9	4	3	8	5	7	1

Puzzle 175

7	5	6	8	1	3	4	9	2
2	8	1	6	4	9	3	5	7
3	4	9	5	2	7	8	1	6
1	6	8	3	9	2	7	4	5
5	7	3	1	8	4	6	2	9
9	2	4	7	6	5	1	8	3
4	1	5	2	7	6	9	3	8
8	3	7	9	5	1	2	6	4
6	9	2	4	3	8	5	7	1

Puzzle 176

3	1	8	6	5	7	4	9	2
9	4	6	1	8	2	3	5	7
7	2	5	9	4	3	8	1	6
6	7	2	5	1	4	9	3	8
1	5	9	7	3	8	2	6	4
8	3	4	2	9	6	5	7	1
2	9	3	8	6	1	7	4	5
4	8	1	3	7	5	6	2	9
5	6	7	4	2	9	1	8	3

Puzzle 177

3	1	8	6	7	5	4	9	2
9	4	6	1	2	8	3	5	7
7	2	5	9	3	4	8	1	6
2	9	3	8	1	6	7	4	5
4	8	1	3	5	7	6	2	9
5	6	7	4	9	2	1	8	3
6	7	2	5	4	1	9	3	8
1	5	9	7	8	3	2	6	4
8	3	4	2	6	9	5	7	1

Puzzle 178

1	8	6	2	4	7	9	3	5
5	3	7	9	1	6	8	4	2
9	4	2	3	8	5	1	7	6
8	5	3	7	6	1	2	9	4
6	9	1	4	2	8	7	5	3
2	7	4	5	9	3	6	1	8
7	6	9	8	3	4	5	2	1
4	2	8	1	5	9	3	6	7
3	1	5	6	7	2	4	8	9

Puzzle 179

4	8	9	1	5	3	6	7	2
3	6	7	2	8	4	1	5	9
5	2	1	6	9	7	8	3	4
9	3	5	8	6	1	2	4	7
8	4	2	3	7	5	9	1	6
1	7	6	4	2	9	3	8	5
2	9	4	5	3	8	7	6	1
7	5	3	9	1	6	4	2	8
6	1	8	7	4	2	5	9	3

Puzzle 180

4	8	9	1	3	5	2	7	6
3	6	7	2	4	8	9	5	1
5	2	1	6	7	9	4	3	8
9	3	5	8	1	6	7	4	2
8	4	2	3	5	7	6	1	9
1	7	6	4	9	2	5	8	3
2	9	4	5	8	3	1	6	7
7	5	3	9	6	1	8	2	4
6	1	8	7	2	4	3	9	5

Puzzle 181

9	4	2	5	6	7	3	8	1
5	3	7	4	8	1	9	2	6
1	8	6	2	9	3	5	4	7
3	9	4	7	2	5	6	1	8
2	1	8	9	4	6	7	5	3
7	6	5	3	1	8	2	9	4
4	5	1	6	7	2	8	3	9
8	7	3	1	5	9	4	6	2
6	2	9	8	3	4	1	7	5

Puzzle 182

6	1	8	2	3	9	5	4	7
7	5	3	4	1	8	9	2	6
2	9	4	5	7	6	3	8	1
5	7	6	3	8	1	2	9	4
8	2	1	9	6	4	7	5	3
4	3	9	7	5	2	6	1	8
1	4	5	6	2	7	8	3	9
3	8	7	1	9	5	4	6	2
9	6	2	8	4	3	1	7	5

Puzzle 183

5	4	1	2	6	7	8	3	9
7	8	3	9	1	5	4	6	2
2	6	9	4	8	3	1	7	5
6	7	5	8	3	1	2	9	4
1	2	8	6	9	4	7	5	3
9	3	4	5	7	2	6	1	8
4	9	2	7	5	6	3	8	1
3	5	7	1	4	8	9	2	6
8	1	6	3	2	9	5	4	7

Puzzle 184

3	9	4	5	2	7	6	1	8
2	1	8	6	4	9	7	5	3
7	6	5	8	1	3	2	9	4
4	5	1	2	7	6	8	3	9
8	7	3	9	5	1	4	6	2
6	2	9	4	3	8	1	7	5
1	8	6	3	9	2	5	4	7
5	3	7	1	8	4	9	2	6
9	4	2	7	6	5	3	8	1

Puzzle 185

3	8	1	2	4	9	5	6	7
9	2	6	7	3	5	4	8	1
5	4	7	6	8	1	2	9	3
2	9	4	5	6	7	3	1	8
7	5	3	8	1	2	9	4	6
6	1	8	4	9	3	7	2	5
1	7	5	9	2	6	8	3	4
4	6	2	3	7	8	1	5	9
8	3	9	1	5	4	6	7	2

Puzzle 186

5	4	7	8	1	6	3	9	2
9	2	6	3	5	7	1	8	4
3	8	1	4	9	2	7	6	5
6	1	8	9	3	4	5	2	7
7	5	3	1	2	8	6	4	9
2	9	4	6	7	5	8	1	3
8	3	9	5	4	1	2	7	6
4	6	2	7	8	3	9	5	1
1	7	5	2	6	9	4	3	8

Puzzle 187

3	9	4	5	2	7	6	1	8
2	1	8	6	4	9	7	5	3
7	6	5	8	1	3	2	9	4
4	5	1	2	7	6	8	3	9
8	7	3	9	5	1	4	6	2
6	2	9	4	3	8	1	7	5
1	8	6	3	9	2	5	4	7
5	3	7	1	8	4	9	2	6
9	4	2	7	6	5	3	8	1

Puzzle 188

3	8	1	2	4	9	5	6	7
9	2	6	7	3	5	4	8	1
5	4	7	6	8	1	2	9	3
2	9	4	5	6	7	3	1	8
7	5	3	8	1	2	9	4	6
6	1	8	4	9	3	7	2	5
1	7	5	9	2	6	8	3	4
4	6	2	3	7	8	1	5	9
8	3	9	1	5	4	6	7	2

Puzzle 189

5	4	7	8	6	1	3	9	2
9	2	6	3	7	5	1	8	4
3	8	1	4	2	9	7	6	5
6	1	8	9	4	3	5	2	7
7	5	3	1	8	2	6	4	9
2	9	4	6	5	7	8	1	3
8	3	9	5	1	4	2	7	6
4	6	2	7	3	8	9	5	1
1	7	5	2	9	6	4	3	8

Puzzle 190

6	7	1	5	8	3	2	9	4
2	4	8	9	6	1	7	5	3
9	5	3	7	2	4	6	1	8
3	8	4	6	7	9	5	2	1
5	1	9	2	4	8	3	6	7
7	6	2	1	3	5	4	8	9
4	2	7	8	1	6	9	3	5
1	9	6	3	5	7	8	4	2
8	3	5	4	9	2	1	7	6

Puzzle 191

7	4	5	8	1	6	3	9	2
6	2	9	3	5	7	1	8	4
1	8	3	4	9	2	7	6	5
3	5	7	1	2	8	6	4	9
4	9	2	6	7	5	8	1	3
8	1	6	9	3	4	5	2	7
5	7	1	2	6	9	4	3	8
2	6	4	7	8	3	9	5	1
9	3	8	5	4	1	2	7	6

Puzzle 192

3	1	8	6	7	5	2	9	4
9	4	6	1	2	8	7	5	3
7	2	5	9	3	4	6	1	8
1	5	9	7	8	3	4	6	2
6	7	2	5	4	1	8	3	9
8	3	4	2	6	9	1	7	5
2	9	3	8	1	6	5	4	7
4	8	1	3	5	7	9	2	6
5	6	7	4	9	2	3	8	1

Puzzle 193

4	1	5	6	7	2	9	3	8
8	3	7	1	5	9	2	6	4
6	9	2	8	3	4	5	7	1
3	4	9	7	2	5	8	1	6
2	8	1	9	4	6	3	5	7
7	5	6	3	1	8	4	9	2
9	2	4	5	6	7	1	8	3
5	7	3	4	8	1	6	2	9
1	6	8	2	9	3	7	4	5

Puzzle 194

6	1	8	7	4	2	5	3	9
7	5	3	6	1	9	2	4	8
2	9	4	5	8	3	6	7	1
5	3	1	2	7	6	9	8	4
8	4	2	9	5	1	7	6	3
9	7	6	4	3	8	1	2	5
3	8	5	1	6	7	4	9	2
4	2	7	3	9	5	8	1	6
1	6	9	8	2	4	3	5	7

Puzzle 195

6	7	5	8	1	3	2	9	4
1	2	8	6	4	9	7	5	3
9	3	4	5	2	7	6	1	8
2	6	9	4	3	8	1	7	5
7	8	3	9	5	1	4	6	2
5	4	1	2	7	6	8	3	9
8	1	6	3	9	2	5	4	7
4	9	2	7	6	5	3	8	1
3	5	7	1	8	4	9	2	6

Puzzle 196

4	1	5	6	7	2	9	3	8
8	3	7	1	5	9	2	6	4
6	9	2	8	3	4	5	7	1
3	4	9	7	2	5	8	1	6
2	8	1	9	4	6	3	5	7
7	5	6	3	1	8	4	9	2
9	2	4	5	6	7	1	8	3
5	7	3	4	8	1	6	2	9
1	6	8	2	9	3	7	4	5

Puzzle 197

6	7	5	8	1	3	2	9	4
1	2	8	6	4	9	7	5	3
9	3	4	5	2	7	6	1	8
2	6	9	4	3	8	1	7	5
7	8	3	9	5	1	4	6	2
5	4	1	2	7	6	8	3	9
3	5	7	1	8	4	9	2	6
8	1	6	3	9	2	5	4	7
4	9	2	7	6	5	3	8	1

Puzzle 198

6	7	5	8	1	3	2	9	4
1	2	8	6	4	9	7	5	3
9	3	4	5	2	7	6	1	8
7	8	3	9	5	1	4	6	2
2	6	9	4	3	8	1	7	5
5	4	1	2	7	6	8	3	9
8	1	6	3	9	2	5	4	7
3	5	7	1	8	4	9	2	6
4	9	2	7	6	5	3	8	1

Puzzle 199

7	5	6	8	1	3	4	9	2
2	8	1	6	4	9	3	5	7
3	4	9	5	2	7	8	1	6
1	6	8	3	9	2	7	4	5
5	7	3	1	8	4	6	2	9
9	2	4	7	6	5	1	8	3
4	1	5	2	7	6	9	3	8
8	3	7	9	5	1	2	6	4
6	9	2	4	3	8	5	7	1

Puzzle 200

9	4	6	1	2	8	3	5	7
3	1	8	6	7	5	4	9	2
7	2	5	9	3	4	8	1	6
6	7	2	5	4	1	9	3	8
1	5	9	7	8	3	2	6	4
8	3	4	2	6	9	5	7	1
2	9	3	8	1	6	7	4	5
4	8	1	3	5	7	6	2	9
5	6	7	4	9	2	1	8	3

Puzzle 201

9	4	6	1	2	8	3	5	7
3	1	8	6	7	5	4	9	2
7	2	5	9	3	4	8	1	6
2	9	3	8	1	6	7	4	5
4	8	1	3	5	7	6	2	9
5	6	7	4	9	2	1	8	3
6	7	2	5	4	1	9	3	8
1	5	9	7	8	3	2	6	4
8	3	4	2	6	9	5	7	1

Puzzle 202

9	2	4	6	7	5	3	1	8
5	7	3	1	2	8	9	4	6
1	6	8	9	3	4	7	2	5
3	8	9	5	4	1	6	7	2
6	4	2	7	8	3	1	5	9
7	1	5	2	6	9	8	3	4
4	5	7	8	1	6	2	9	3
2	9	6	3	5	7	4	8	1
8	3	1	4	9	2	5	6	7

Puzzle 203

8	1	3	5	7	6	2	9	4
6	4	9	8	2	1	7	5	3
5	2	7	4	3	9	6	1	8
9	5	1	3	8	7	4	6	2
2	7	6	1	4	5	8	3	9
4	3	8	9	6	2	1	7	5
3	9	2	6	1	8	5	4	7
1	8	4	7	5	3	9	2	6
7	6	5	2	9	4	3	8	1

Puzzle 204

8	1	3	2	9	4	5	7	6
6	4	9	7	5	3	8	2	1
5	2	7	6	1	8	4	3	9
9	5	1	4	6	2	3	8	7
2	7	6	8	3	9	1	4	5
4	3	8	1	7	5	9	6	2
3	9	2	5	4	7	6	1	8
1	8	4	9	2	6	7	5	3
7	6	5	3	8	1	2	9	4

Puzzle 205

7	6	5	4	9	2	3	1	8
1	8	4	3	5	7	9	6	2
3	9	2	8	1	6	5	7	4
5	2	7	9	3	4	6	8	1
6	4	9	1	2	8	7	3	5
8	1	3	6	7	5	2	4	9
2	7	6	5	4	1	8	9	3
9	5	1	7	8	3	4	2	6
4	3	8	2	6	9	1	5	7

Puzzle 206

4	5	7	8	1	6	3	9	2
2	9	6	3	5	7	1	8	4
8	3	1	4	9	2	7	6	5
1	6	8	9	3	4	5	2	7
5	7	3	1	2	8	6	4	9
9	2	4	6	7	5	8	1	3
3	8	9	5	4	1	2	7	6
6	4	2	7	8	3	9	5	1
7	1	5	2	6	9	4	3	8

Puzzle 207

8	3	9	5	1	4	2	7	6
4	6	2	7	3	8	9	5	1
1	7	5	2	9	6	4	3	8
6	1	8	9	4	3	5	2	7
7	5	3	1	8	2	6	4	9
2	9	4	6	5	7	8	1	3
5	4	7	8	6	1	3	9	2
9	2	6	3	7	5	1	8	4
3	8	1	4	2	9	7	6	5

Printed in the United States
by Baker & Taylor Publisher Services